An Odyssey in War and Peace

OTHER LOTUS TITLES

Ajit Bhattacharjea	*Sheikh Mohammad Abdullah: Tragic Hero of Kashmir*
Amarinder Singh	*The Last Sunset: The Rise and Fall of the Lahore Durbar*
Anil Dharker	*Icons: Men & Women Who Shaped Today's India*
Aitzaz Ahsan	*The Indus Saga: The Making of Pakistan*
Alam Srinivas & TR Vivek	*IPL: The Inside Story*
Amir Mir	*The True Face of Jehadis: Inside Pakistan's Terror Networks*
Ashok Mitra	*The Starkness of It*
Dr Humanyun Khan & G. Parthasarthy	*Diplomatic Divide*
Gyanendra Pandey & Yunus Samad	*Faultlines of Nationhood*
H.L.O. Garrett	*The Trial of Bahadur Shah Zafar*
M.J. Akbar	*India: The Siege Within*
M.J. Akbar	*Kashmir: Behind the Vale*
M.J. Akbar	*The Shade of Swords*
M.J. Akbar	*Byline*
M.J. Akbar	*Blood Brothers: A Family Saga*
Maj. Gen. Ian Cardozo	*Param Vir: Our Heroes in Battle*
Maj. Gen. Ian Cardozo	*The Sinking of INS Khukri: What Happened in 1971*
Madhu Trehan	*Tehelka as Metaphor*
Mushirul Hasan	*India Partitioned. 2 Vols*
Mushirul Hasan	*John Company to the Republic*
Mushirul Hasan	*Knowledge, Power and Politics*
Nayantara Sahgal (ed.)	*Before Freedom: Nehru's Letters to His Sister*
Nilima Lambah	*A Life Across Three Continents*
Robert Hutchison	*The Raja of Harsil: The Legend of Frederick 'Pahari' Wilson*
Sharmishta Gooptu and Boria Majumdar (eds)	*Revisiting 1857: Myth, Memory, History*
Shashi Joshi	*The Last Durbar*
Shashi Tharoor & Shaharyar M. Khan	*Shadows across the Playing Field*
Shrabani Basu	*Spy Princess: The Life of Noor Inayat Khan*
Shyam Bhatia	*Goodbye Shahzadi: A Political Biography*
Thomas Weber	*Gandhi, Gandhism and the Gandhians*
Zubin Mehta	*The Score of My Life*

FORTHCOMING TITLES

Masood Hyder	*State Under Pressure*
Jaiwant Paul	*Heroes and Villains of 1857*

An Odyssey in War and Peace

An Autobiography

Lt Gen. J.F.R. Jacob

LOTUS COLLECTION
ROLI BOOKS

First impression May 2011
Second impression August 2011

First published in India in 2011
The Lotus Collection
An imprint of
Roli Books Pvt. Ltd
M-75, Greater Kailash II Market
New Delhi 110 048
Phone: ++91 (011) 4068 2000
Fax: ++91 (011) 2921 7185
E-mail: info@rolibooks.com; Website: www.rolibooks.com

Also at
Bangalore, Chennai & Mumbai

Cover: Bonita Vaz-Shimray
Production: Shaji Sahadevan

ISBN: 978-81-7436-840-9

Typeset in Adobe Caslon Pro by Roli Books Pvt Ltd
and printed at Rakmo Press Pvt. Ltd New Delhi

CONTENTS

Dedicated to

Gen. P.P. Kumaramangalam
DSO MBE
A great soldier, human being, and friend. Had it not been for him, I would have resigned from the Army.

Preface

It has been a tempestuous journey that is drawing to a close. There were the years of the sword from 1941 when I joined the army to August 1978 when I retired as Army Commander Eastern Command. I learnt my soldiering during the Second World War, both in the deserts of the Middle East and the dense jungle-clad ridges and mangrove swamps of the Arakan in Burma. Immediately after the Japanese surrender we were engaged in highly unpopular counter-insurgency operations in Sumatra, aimed at restoring Dutch rule there.

After Independence, I returned to India from a gunnery staff course of instruction in England to the Artillery School in Deolali. The British were leaving and as the only other senior Indian officer there I had to take over the school from the British and also to divide the assets of the school between India and Pakistan.

This was followed by a period of peace-time soldiering.

In 1969, I was ordered to conduct operations to drive the Naxalites out of West Bengal. This was followed by counter-insurgency operations in the North-East (NE) leading to the signing of the Shillong Accord in 1975. The operations conducted in Mizoram influenced their leaders to come to Calcutta for the Calcutta Conference to discuss the modalities of peace.

The campaign in December 1971, in East Pakistan, led to the unconditional public surrender of 93,000 troops of the Pakistan

Eastern Command, the only public surrender in history. To quote the Pakistan National Defence College study of the war:

> The Indians planned and executed their offensive in a textbook manner. It was a classic example of through planning, minute coordination and bold execution. The credit clearly goes to General Jacob's meticulous preparations in the Indian Eastern command and to the implementation by his corps commanders.

Niazi had proposed a ceasefire and a hand-over of the government to the United Nations (UN) with guarantees of no reprisals etc. There was no mention of India. The ceasefire proposed by Niazi was rejected outright by Bhutto who vowed to fight on. The end result was an unconditional public surrender, the only one in history. The Hamood ur Rehman Commission of Enquiry asked Gen. Niazi: 'Gen. Niazi, when you had 26,400 troops in Dacca and the Indians a few thousand outside and you could have fought on for at least two more weeks. The UN was in session [Polish resolution] and had you fought on for even one more day the Indians would have had to go back: why did you accept a shameful unconditional public surrender and provide a guard of honour commanded by your ADC?' Niazi replied that he was compelled to do so by Gen. Jacob who blackmailed him into surrendering. This he has repeated in his book *Betrayal of East Pakistan*. After the surrender of 93,000 Pakistani troops, India emerged as a regional superpower. I have often wondered, what would have happened had I failed to convert the proposed ceasefire under the auspices of the UN into an unconditional surrender? We would have had to return the very next day.

In my book *Surrender at Dacca: Birth of a Nation* (1997), I had given an objective account of the operations in East Pakistan in 1971. The book has been translated into Chinese, Thai, Persian, Arabic, Hebrew, and Bengali. I had given copies both to Field Marshal Manekshaw and Lt Gen. Jagjit Aurora in 1997. There were no rejoinders from them. The book is studied in many military institutions abroad and also some universities.

The waging of war is a complex business involving almost all sections of the population. The conduct and progress of military operations is far from smooth and never wholly predictable. The successful conduct of operations depends upon imaginative planning, flexibility, and the ability to react rapidly. It is imperative that one is not overtaken by events. Mobility and manoeuvre are essential ingredients.

Military operations require proper infrastructural and logistical backing. The establishment of the infrastructure and building up the logistics were factors crucial to our successful operations in 1971. Once operations commenced, our troops did not have to look back. Everything was in place.

Politics, like war, is a complex business. My tenure as governor in Goa was very eventful. Politics in Goa is something like musical chairs. Legislators frequently switch loyalties. In the period of around six months when I was there I saw four governments. This was followed by a spell of four months of President's rule and the installation of an elected government.

My tour of duty in Punjab was less tempestuous. Most of my energies were devoted to administering the city of Chandigarh.

Today, the Naxalite insurgency is escalating. The police and paramilitary are unable to handle it. A pragmatic Mrs Indira Gandhi knew what to do. She ordered the army in 1969 to drive them out of West Bengal. Unfortunately the government, due to pressures from the states concerned, is hesitant to use the armed forces. However, some recent acts of violence which have claimed many lives, including those of civilians, has forced the government to think afresh, and in all likelihood the armed forces are likely to be involved in anti-naxal operations in some manner in the near future.

The Naxals are said to be getting money and weapons from China and are linking up with the Marxists in Nepal. The Naxal insurgency is escalating and may soon get out of control.

Pakistan is continuing its efforts to destabilize our country. Their terrorist activities in India are on the increase. 26/11 will almost certainly be followed by other terrorist acts. Infiltration and terrorist acts in Jammu & Kashmir are also vehicles used by Pakistan to destabilize India and to drain our resources. Pakistan views India to be its paramount threat. Both Pakistan and China are colluding to destabilize India.

China too is stepping up its propaganda and increasing its activities in the border regions. The infrastructure in Tibet is being built up with the construction of roads, railway lines and airfields. China can, within weeks, deploy up to 30 divisions in Tibet.

We do not have sufficient divisions in the NE and Ladakh. Our divisions there lack adequate firepower and mobility. Our air force needs to deploy many more squadrons. The infrastructure in the NE needs to be upgraded. We are also committed to defending Bhutan. The government had agreed to raise two more mountain divisions. At least four more divisions are required for the defence of Ladakh, the NE and Bhutan. The building up of the infrastructure and the raising of divisions should be accelerated. In addition, our military also needs an induction of modern weapon systems.

Meanwhile, the Chinese dragon continues to breathe fire, reminding us of what happened in 1962. Government must not blink: they must stand firm and not buckle under their threats.

In sum, we are surrounded by hostile neighbours: Pakistan in the west, China in the north, and an emerging Maoist-influenced Nepal. Bangladesh is fortunately trying to curb ISI-sponsored insurgents from being inducted into the NE and the cities of India.

It is necessary to strengthen our relations with Russia. In 1971, it was the Treaty of Peace and Friendship with the Soviet Union conceived by Mrs Indira Gandhi and the subsequent movement of some 40 Soviet army divisions to the Sinjiang and 7 to the Manchurian borders that deterred the Chinese from intervening in East Pakistan.

Our relations with the United States, due largely to the efforts of Prime Minister Dr Manmohan Singh and former Presidents George Bush and Barack Obama are being upgraded. These relations have advanced a long way from the hostile environment that existed during the Nixon and Kissinger years.

The road ahead is rocky and strewn with obstacles. Hopefully, the government will find the strength to face the challenges and pressures from the Pakistan-China axis.

Writing an autobiographical account is never easy as it is difficult for the writer to decide what should go in and what should not. There is also the problem of emotions affecting objectivity. Here, I wish to gratefully acknowledge the contribution of my editor Tapan K. Ghosh, who discussed the material with me at length from the point of view of the reader. He went through the copy meticulously and helped me to maintain focus and balance. Finally, I am indebted to my publishers for taking up this project and bringing out the book on a priority basis.

Lt Gen. J.F.R. Jacob

1

The Early Years

I was born in Calcutta, or Kolkata as it is now known, a beautiful and cultured city. This was the Calcutta of the late 1920s, a vibrant city bathed in a myriad colours after dark. The city welcomed migrants and people from distant lands with open arms, a quality it continues to enjoy to this day. Many Jewish families had come to Calcutta from Baghdad some 200 years earlier. There were two other Jewish communities in India, in Cochin and Mumbai, which had come some 2,000 years earlier. My great-grandmother left Syria some 200 years ago and travelled to India via Iraq, Persia, and Afghanistan to Multan. My grandmother, some time later, moved from Multan to Calcutta where my mother Carrie was born.

My parents were deeply religious people and maintained a strict Kosher regime at the table. I remember being scolded once for using the cutlery intended for milk dishes to eat a meat dish.

Our family used to attend our synagogue, the Bethel, on high holidays. We had four permanent benches in the synagogue which now lie unoccupied. We were reasonably well off; I remember a large house on Loudon Street, two horse buggies, and two cars. My other brothers, Maurice, Eric, and I used to cycle to the Botanical Gardens and would sometimes catch the ferry from Prinsep Ghat to the pier at Botanical Gardens. We loved the great banyan tree there, wandered around the Jain temple, Victoria Memorial (rowing on the pond there), and played games on the maidan and in Fort William. We flew kites from the roof which was great fun, cutting and capturing rival kites. We enjoyed the buggy rides to the lakes and the rowing there. I remember saving our pocket money to buy cakes at Nahoums in New Market. One of our favourite places was the National Museum. We sat on Theebaw's huge Burma teak throne which was returned to Burma by Lord Louis Mountbatten in 1947. We were fascinated by the Egyptian section and the sculptures down the ages.

There were many movie theatres in the city: Globe, New Empire, Metro, Regal, and the newly built Lighthouse. During our winter school holidays we saw many movies, including the *Wizard of OZ, China Seas*, Clark Gable`s *Gone with the Wind*, and *Mutiny on the Bounty*. Matinee tickets in the mid-stalls then cost nine annas, and it stretched our pocket money to buy tickets.

My parents engaged a Hebrew teacher for us. My elder brother Maurice was diligent and proficient in the language, and today I greatly regret that I cut classes.

We played with brightly painted tops made of hard guava wood, sharpened their spikes to shatter those of the other boys. Yo-yos were the craze then and we learnt to perform many tricks with them.

In the late 1930s many Jewish refugees arrived in Calcutta, and my family helped to look after a few of them. My father ran his own business; he spoke very little about it, speaking instead of his earlier days in Gorakhpur. It appears he had an indigo plantation there and came to Calcutta when German synthetic dyes supplanted Indigo.

My father met with an accident and was for a long time a patient at Presidency General Hospital. My mother was preoccupied with looking after him and could not cope. We boys, i.e. my elder brother Maurice, my younger brother Eric, and I, were all packed off to boarding school, Victoria, located some 6,000 feet up in the Darjeeling hills. We were sorry to leave home for boarding school, and hearing that the term extended to nine months, from March up to the end of November,s were apprehensive of what lay ahead.

Boarding School

The Darjeeling Mail train chugged along from Silliguri, puffing and panting up the steep gradients. It was 2 March 1932. A grinning

Nepalese boy sat on the bumper of the engine, throwing sand on the rails to prevent the wheels from slipping. The train criss-crossed the cart road, and progress was slow, painfully slow. Children ran alongside, whooping and laughing. They looked so different, Nepalese, Bhutia, and Lepcha, their faces wreathed in smiles. I gazed in awe at the snow-capped mountains; my first view of the mighty ranges of the Himalaya. We passed tea estates with manicured tea bushes, forests of teak, and the tall *Cryptomaria japonica*. The train stopped at every little station: places like Sukhna and the railway workshop complex at Tindharia. We steamed slowly into Kurseong to be met by bevies of young boys and girls jostling with one another to carry our luggage up the hill to our school: Victoria.

I got my first glimpse of the school nestling amidst the forests which was to be my second home for the next eight years. The building was imposing, built on a flat terrace some 250 yard long. Some 200 feet below it was another terrace scarped out of the hill, and this was where the cricket and hockey grounds were located. The athletics field had the distinction of having a 220-yard straight track. There were three houses, Mallory, Irvine, and Kellas, named after Everest heroes. Everest itself was not visible from the school but the Kanchenjunga massif was visible on a clear day. It was fascinating watching its hues at dawn, and especially at sunset glowing pink and deepening to deep red and purple.

The school term was nine months long; too long. We got a short break in October for the Puja holidays, and, then there was a long break of three months, December through February, between terms. I have mixed feelings regarding my schooldays. On the plus side, the teachers were mostly English, some competent, some not. It was fortunate that I was able to top my form year after year, winning most of the prizes. Our day began with physical training. Games were compulsory; I played cricket, hockey, rugby, football, and a little tennis. I managed to graduate from the fifth eleven to the first eleven in hockey. I joined the cadet wing of the Northern Bengal Mounted Rifles (NBMR), a territorial army unit and looked forward to the weekly parades and the opportunity to participate in the musketry practice. We trained on the Lee Enfield rifle and the Lewis gun. I was part of the team that won the Baker Musketry Shield for three consecutive years, from 1937 to 1939. The practice sessions were difficult: 100, 300, and 600 yards. My exposure to the Northern Bengal Mounted Rifles made me yearn to join the army. On the negative side, there was an undercurrent of anti-Semitism in school. Two of the staff did little to conceal their feelings. Some of the boys too shared these sentiments and sometimes this led to blows, but I was fortunately able to hold my own. Surprisingly, I found the Anglican Chaplain G.B. Elliot to be the most sympathetic and supportive. He often invited me to his quarters for afternoon tea and introduced me to Western classical music; Brahms, Beethoven, Mozart, and Elgar formed part of his collection. He never ever spoke to me about religion. He offered me toffees with the words 'Jackie have one'. He later became chaplain of the prestigious Saint Paul's Cathedral in Calcutta and did much to vitalize the Anglican community in the city. I will always cherish his kindness and compassion.

The school was set amidst virgin forests, and we were allowed the freedom to roam the forests. I got to love the forested hills and valleys, the lichens, the ferns, and the gushing *jhora*s (mountain streams). Throughout my school years my buddy was Desmond Doig, and together we explored the forests and scrambled up the *jhora*s right up to their source. We often descended from the school, which was at an elevation of some 6000 feet, to the Balasan river and Kettle valley some 4000 feet below. On one of our treks we ran into a portly, cassocked figure, bamboo staff in hand. It was Father Prior of the Oxford Mission, rambling down the narrow forest trails singing 'Roll pumpkin, roll pumpkin, I've biscuits and cherries, the stones I throw out thus'. He had no cherries but offered biscuits to us famished boys.

As I mentioned, we got a break of fifteen days for the Puja holidays. In 1938, Doig and I approached Sir Basil Gould, the British resident in Sikkim based at Sikkim House, for a permit to go into the Chumbi Valley in Tibet. Sir Basil was most courteous, invited us for lunch, and wished us a happy journey. I wonder whether school kids today would be so received at Sikkim House, the present Raj Bhawan. We crossed groups of yaks moving to new grazing areas, and surprisingly an elderly missionary lady trudging along, staff in hand, wearing a sola topee with veil, who gave us some *churpi* (yak milk toffee). We returned via Jelap la along the Younghusband trail.

Many years later, in 1943 during the war, I had to travel to the Arakan from Delhi. The train was absolutely packed. Walking down the platform I saw a man in Sikkimese attire outside a four-berth compartment. My luck was in. Sir Basil Gould was travelling to Calcutta. I explained my predicament and he offered me the other lower berth. He then had a wire sent to Mughal Sarai station for a special dinner He then autographed his *Tibetan Word Book* for me, which regrettably I subsequently lost. Gould was indeed a gentleman diplomat, and administrator.

I appeared for the Senior Cambridge school certificate in 1938, topped in the country, and was awarded a scholarship. I spent a year of college at Victoria in 1939, moving in 1940 to Saint Xavier's College, Calcutta. I was thrilled to be back in Calcutta, the city of my birth. Jews from Iraq had migrated to the city around 1780; fleeing persecution they were well accepted there, prospered, and contributed much to society and charity. Jews in India never encountered any anti-semetism from Indians.

Calcutta is a city I love. As kids we wandered and cycled almost everywhere, even up to Chandernagore which was then very French. I had a school friend there, the son of a defrocked catholic priest.

War clouds were looming. I was appalled at the Nazi invasions and atrocities. Jewish refugees began arriving in Calcutta in large numbers, and my family helped in whatever manner they could. I then made up my mind to go and fight, influenced by the writings of the war poets, especially A.E. Housman, Julian Grenfell, Siegfried Sasson, Rupert Brooke, Wilfred Owen, and Herbert Read. My parents were however keen that I should continue studying for the master's degree. I kept my own counsel till my orders to join the army were received.

Incidentally, both my brothers were also subsequently to get involved in the war. In 1942, Maurice was commissioned in 2 Punjab and served in Burma throughout the war. After the war, he was demobilized in England, where he held a responsible position in the law courts. Eric joined the air force towards the end of the war and thereafter he too moved to England and joined an industrial unit in a technical capacity.

2

Off to the Second World War

I decided to join the army in mid-1941. I knew Fort William in Calcutta quite well as I had some school friends there: Tich Brogan and Burnett. I pedalled my bicycle through Plassey gate for an interview with the commander of the Garrison, Maj. Gen. Heydeman. The interview went off well until we came to the matter of relevant papers. He said as my documents were not complete, I should come back with them. As I began walking out, disappointed, he called me back, saying that as I was so keen to join, I could do so. Another interview followed at the summer headquarters of the Indian Army at Simla. The interview was conducted by a board of British Indian Army gabardine-clad brass hats. There was also a pompous ruler of one of the smaller Indian states on the board. I was asked a couple of questions by the general presiding over the board. The royal personage then asked me, 'Do you shoot games?' I was taken aback for a few seconds, not getting his meaning, and then shot back, 'No sir, I don't shoot games, I shoot goals'. There were peals of laughter allround and no further questions. I took my leave and walked out. It seemed incredible that with the war in Europe at a critical stage, Army Headquarters was still oriented to such a peace environment. This complacency was to be shattered by Pearl Harbour and the Japanese invasion of Malaya and Burma.

On my way back to Calcutta I stopped off at Delhi to meet a friend at Lady Irwin College. We used to meet in the principal Dr Hannah Sen's bungalow in Sundar Nagar. I was serious about this girl, and her mother too was keen on my marrying her. Later, after some dating, in 1952 I was being posted to an inaccessible area in Kashmir for some three years. The girl did not want to wait that long and so it ended, but we continued to remain in touch.

I broke journey again at Agra to see the Taj Mahal. In those days the minarets were open to the public. I took a number of photographs from the top of a minaret with my Kodak Brownie box camera. On reaching the base I discovered that my pocket had been picked. My railway ticket was in the wallet, so all I was left with was some small change. I was at a loss to know what to do. The station master was sympathetic, and said that he would ensure that up to Mughal Sarai, where his jurisdiction ended, I would not be asked to produce my ticket but after that I would be on my own. I locked myself in a coupé, and despite some banging on the door at various stations, reached Howrah station, Calcutta, without any trouble, rushed quickly through the exit barrier, and made it home. After a few weeks my orders arrived to report to the officers' training school at Mhow. I had much explaining to do as no one at home had been aware of my intention to join the army. When, however, I explained that I was going to fight the Nazis, they were reconciled and gave me their blessings.

The officers' training school was hastily set up in Mhow cantonment in central India. It was from Mhow that in 1857, General Sir Hugh Rose assembled a force from the Bombay Army to march on the Rani of Jhansi. The terrain around Mhow was very suitable for the conduct of military training. The training schedules were tough and demanding. However, off parade we were treated as officers, comfortably quartered, and provided with personal servants. Our company commander was of the old school of the British Indian Army. During our long route marches, we resented the way he rode alongside astride a splendid charger. On one occasion he had organized an ambush en route. When it was over he asked us if we were aware of the persons who were in the ambush, and we replied in the negative. We were thunderstruck by his reply: 'I did not expect you to notice; remember a good soldier looks only to his front; march on!'. Some two years later, in the Mayu range in the Arakan, he was commanding a battalion supported by my battery. I reminded him of his remarks which he laughed off.

Training to be a Gunner

I was summoned to the company office and told that I was to volunteer for the artillery. I replied that my first choice had been the infantry and as I was doing very well, I should get my first choice. The reply was sharp: 'You have now volunteered for the artillery and will go there: *march out*.' The artillery was not a popular choice in those days as it meant an additional period of training and commissioning some months later than those in the other branches of the army. The artillery school had the reputation of failing and returning a large percentage of the trainees. The few who were selected were given a short period of leave prior to reporting to the artillery school at Deolali.

Deolali in those days was a small two-company cantonment which became well-known throughout the army for its mental hospital. The term 'Deolali tap' was coined here to refer to a soldier who was mentally deranged. Sadly, Mental Hospital Road on which it was located was later renamed. The trains stopped at Deolali for two minutes, just sufficient to take out one's baggage. The centrepiece of the platform was an antique James Macabe clock. There were no taxis to move one's baggage, the local tongas being the only means of transportation. The artillery school had moved to Deolali from Kakul in 1940. After Mhow, its infrastructure was sorely inadequate. We were housed four to a sparsely furnished tent. The tents were not electrified, so we had to study by the light of a hurricane lamp. We were to undertake a crash course of seven weeks under instructors with little experience of teaching. The officer-in-charge was from the Reserve, a 'boxwalla' (businessman) from a Calcutta jute mill, assisted by a bombardier from a British field artillery regiment. We learnt very little and were constantly shouted at and berated: '*You will never make a gunner!*'. We were given little respite or time for recreation, our off hours generally being occupied with extra gun drill. There were originally 28 cadets in our course, and of these seven were reverted to other arms and services. There was no passing out parade or function. On 7 June 1942, I donned the badges of the rank of a second lieutenant.

I had volunteered for an operational assignment in the Middle East. The regiment I was earmarked for (1st Indian Anti-tank Regiment) was engaged in battle in Bir Hachiem in the western desert of north Africa. I boarded a troopship at Bombay, which was diverted to Basra upstream of the Shatt-el Arab in Iraq. I off-loaded my kit and proceeded to the transit camp at Shaiba for further directions. I reported to the officer commanding, a major of the Scinde Horse, a tank regiment of the Indian Army. He had a ruddy face, bulging eyes, and his blue veins were prominently visible. He asked me to deposit the three-day's rations which he said I should have brought with me from the ship. I replied that I was unaware of this proviso and that I had not brought any. He retorted that if that was the case I would not get food for three days. I moved my baggage to an adjacent tent and returned to the mess tent.

There was a shout-out taking place between a major of a British anti-tank regiment and the camp commandant. The gunner major demanded that the gunners who were accompanying him be fed, but to no avail. He then told the camp commandant that if they were not fed, he would place the commandant under arrest. In the ensuing bedlam I quietly went to the dining tent, had my dinner, and retired to my tent which was set amidst a number of unoccupied ones. A dust storm began to blow and sleep was fitfull.

I had a feeling I was not alone. When I got out in the morning the surrounding unoccupied tents had been removed, apparently during the dust storm. An organized gang had removed them, loaded them on to some parked trucks, and driven them off. I went to the camp office to get my movement order. The commandant, Major Vosper, then ordered me to disburse pay to the British other ranks, pushing a stack of dinars towards me. When I began counting them, he sarcastically remarked that there was no need at all for me to do so as he had himself checked them. After paying out I was one hundred dinars short (one dinar then was equivalent to one pound sterling). I returned to the office and apprised the commandant. He retorted, 'You should have bloody well counted them before you left; don't waste my time!'.

I was told to report to Headquarters, Artillery, in Baghdad. I travelled to Baghdad with others by rail in cattle flats, contracting sandfly fever en route. I was admitted to a British military hospital near Baghdad which had earlier been a palace. The hospital was well run. I vividly recall the daily visit of the commanding officer, preceded by the regimental sergeant major who, with a loud and shattering roar, announced the arrival of the brigadier doctor. We were expected to sit up to attention in our beds whilst this dignitary passed through, nodding condescendingly at each one of us. After a week I was discharged from hospital.

I reported to Headquarters, Artillery, and was told to report to my regiment, the 1st Indian Anti-Tank Regiment, elements of which were returning from the western desert. I travelled to Haifa along the pipeline to find them but later joined up with the regiment at Kifri in northern Iraq along with other units of 8 Indian Division. A new commanding officer Lt Col John Daniells had just taken over the regiment which was in the process of re-forming. I was given command of a troop of guns. The troop was affiliated to 1/5 Royal Gurkha Rifles commanded by Lt Col Briggs. Briggs, or 'Briggo' as he was known, was hard of hearing which was a source of embarrassment because this meant that he was not fully capable of taking down orders and relied on me to do so.

There were reports that a German army group under Field Marshal Erich von Manstein was planning to move through the Caucasus to capture the oilfields at Kirkuk. I was sent to reconnoitre areas for defence positions. The terrain was rugged and breathtaking, and involved our crossing fast-flowing rivers, the Greater and Lesser Zabs.

The politics of the region was dominated by the Anglo-French rivalries for the division of the Ottoman Empire. This figured in the correspondence of Mc Mahon-Hussain pledging a new Arab state. This was followed in 1916 by a proposal drawn up by Sir Mark Sykes of Britain's MI 6 and Georges Picot of France which proposed dividing the Ottoman Empire into British and French zones of influence. They also envisioned an Arab coalition or confederation of Arab states. A separate state for the Kurds was at one time considered but shelved. Russia was to be given freedom to acquire some Armenian provinces as well as sizeable Kurdish territory. After the overthrow of the Czar in 1917, the Soviets withdrew from the agreement. The provisions of this agreement were modified at the

San Remo conference of 1920-2. The Arabs did not get what they were promised. The seeds of future conflict and instability in the Middle East that we see to this day were sown in the Sykes-Picot Agreement.

During my reconnaissance, I was accompanied by a detachment of 1/5 Royal Gurkha Rifles. Our rations were unappetizing and meagre. Fortunately, the Gurkhas were invariably able, with the aid of mosquito nets, to provide us with fish.

The German offensive through the Caucacus did not materialize as Hitler diverted his forces to back his attempts to capture Stalingrad.

Early Lessons in Man Management

The British officers in the early days of the war were gentlemen from upper class families. My battery commander was Major Dick Peters, a territorial army officer who in civil life was a solicitor and the local squire. He was considerate and approachable. The battery Captain, Norman Harding, was, in civil life, a jeweller. I learnt a great deal from them, particularly in terms of man management.

One lesson was driven home regarding man management. I had given a task to be carried out by my troop leader, a Viceroy Commissioned Officer (VCO) Ghulam Mohammed. The task was not completed; I scolded him in front of the men. The VCO protested to my battery commander that his *izzat* had been compromised. *Izzat* means honour and much more. There is no equivalent in any other language (a person who loses his *izzat* loses face and respect). My battery commander called me and said, 'Jacko [by the name I was known], how old are you?' 'Nineteen,' I replied. 'Jacko,' he said, 'this VCO has 24 years service, many more years than your age. That will be all.' I never forgot this rebuke from Maj. Dick Peters.

I got to know the men in my troop, the villages they came from, details of their family, and their problems. Man management is one of the most essential ingredients of successful command, but this aspect unfortunately today does not receive the importance it deserves.

Service conditions were tough and our tented accommodation was very basic and rations even more, although this was supplemented by hunting. We were out on training most of the time. We took part in exercises with Glubb Pasha's Arab Legion. Located nearby at Khanaquin was the Polish Carpathian division commanded by General Wladyslaw Anders. The Polish soldiers had trickled in from Poland through Central Asia and Persia. I met Anders, a most imposing man. He told me he would fight his way back to Poland. Unfortunately for him, at the end of the Second World War the Soviets refused to let him return to Poland.

The regiment could not get the required reinforcements nor equipment as these were not available in the theatre. It was therefore ordered to return to India to re-form. We were very disappointed as we were keen to stay on with 8th Indian Division, a crack division commanded by a colourful, competent, and popular general, Maj. Gen. Dudley Russell 'Pasha'. After Independence in 1947, he was appointed as adviser to General K.M. Cariappa but Cariappa declined to avail of his expertise. In 1950, when I was assigned to the general staff at Army Headquarters, I approached Russell 'Pasha', as he was popularly known, several times for advice. He was always courteous and helpful. He spoke to me of his experiences in the war; one in particular I would like to recall. 8th Indian Division was to be assigned the task of carrying out an assault on the Island of Cos. The thinking of the theatre command was that, as the numbers of Italian and German troops defending the Island were equal, they would counter-balance each other and as such the planned operation should present no difficulty. The admiral commanding the task force that was to support the assault then turned round to Russell, the soldier who was to execute the plan. Russell's reply was indeed classic, 'Gentlemen I stopped reading the brothers Grimm at the age of ten'. The operation was called off.

We were originally scheduled to move back to India by the land route. We were all looking forward to this but it was not to be. We were then ordered to hand over our vehicles and move to India by sea. We landed at Karachi and proceeded by train to Sialkot, then a tidy compact cantonment. We collected our equipment, vehicles, guns, and mortars, and instead of going back to the Middle East we were allotted to 26th Indian Division which was about to move to the Arakan in Burma. After a short spell of jungle training in the Ranchi area, we moved to the Arakan. 26th Division was part of XV

Corps commanded by Lt Gen. Bill Slim, but he was soon promoted to command XIV Army. Lt Gen. Sir Philip Christison assumed command of XV Corps. The newly raised 26th Indian Division was commanded by Maj. Gen. C.E.N. Lomax. Slim had been extremely popular in the corps and frequently visited the troops. I particularly remember one occasion when I was giving a demonstration on bunker busting in the presence of a large number of officers, including Lt Gen. Bill Slim, the corps commander. In my eagerness I forgot to dig in the spades of the gun, which on firing recoiled, the telescope hitting me and giving me a black eye. Slim was sympathetic, saying, 'Easy does it'.

Here I must narrate another incident that related to the importance of man management. We were located for training, prior to our departure for Arakan, at Milestone 13, Lohadaga Road. A battalion of the Bombay Grenadiers was located at Milestone 11. Orders were issued from Delhi for the reorganization of the class composition of the unit. This was resented by the men, who refused to implement the orders. The British officers of the unit over-reacted and called it a mutiny and left the unit area.

My commanding officer Lt Col 'Pip' Lascelles was ordered to handle the situation, and artillery was deployed. Lascelles called me and said, 'Jacko, go do something there'. I drove to the unit lines where the men were gathered on the sports ground. I met the subedar major and other viceroy commissioned officers. Long discussions took place. I promised that if they went back to work I would ensure that no action was taken against them. Reluctantly they returned to their duties and I reported back and briefed Lt Col Lascelles. I stressed that I had given assurances on behalf of the corps commander and my word of honour that no action would be taken against them. That was the end of the matter.

In the Thick of Action

Our regiment moved to the Arakan and took part with the 26th Indian Division in operations along Mayu Range. The regiment was complimented by Gen. Lomax on its performance. I was wounded in the operations during which Japanese Zeros straffed and bombed us in Burma. I vividly recall a Zero swooping down towards me and the face of the Japanese pilot. In a burst of frustrated anger I fired my revolver at him to little effect! There were many casualties in that attack. The surgeon in the field ambulance did a good quick job on me and I was soon back in circulation.

During a lull in operations I went on a short trek to Sikkim with Capt. Douglas Hume of our regiment. The commanding officer was surprised when told of our itinerary as the others who went on leave preferred to socialize in Calcutta.

Lt Robin Mirrlees, son of Maj. Gen. Ray Mirrlees, the director of artillery at Delhi, was my gun position officer (GPO). The GPO works out the data to engage the target. Ray Mirrlees had been Montgomery's artillery commander before being assigned to the India command. He had the reputation of being fiery and short-tempered. Robin, on the other hand, was more interested in literature and poetry than soldiering.

We took part in several operations along the Mayu range. I had one very narrow escape. I was officiating commander of the battery and was moving with my signaller and OP assistant to relieve the OP detachment. We apparently lost our way in the jungle and stopped at a jungle clearing. After a few minutes I was able to fix our position, but from the other end of the clearing a few Japanese emerged. They stopped and took up positions, and my assistant fired at them. We then slipped back into the jungle, and after a few minutes when I felt that the Japanese were near our last position, I called down artillery fire on the spot we had just left. I gave the following order: 'Battery target, battery target, grid reference ... fire by order five rounds gunfire.' After a minute or so I ordered: 'Fire'. After the rounds landed, I ordered a repeat. We succeeded in reaching our OP.

The regiment was earmarked for amphibious operations. My battery, which was operating independently, was to move to the beach at Ukhia, south of Cox's Bazaar, to train for amphibious operations. As I had to go ahead, I asked Robin to bring the main body of the battery to Ukhia and that I would place guides short of it. Robin was really incredible: I had, on one occasion, tried to stop him trying to strike a cobra with a copy of Willats' *Roman Urdu!*. Robin, leading the battery and reading a book, instead of turning north when they reached Arakan road from the Mayu range, turned south towards the Japanese positions. Fortunately there was a check-post manned by military police and a single strand of barbed wire across the dirt road. The military police with difficulty managed to turn the vehicles 180° around on a very narrow path of wooden planks.

Much as I liked Robin, it was difficult for me to keep him in the battery and asked Lascelles to move him out. He responded, 'Jacko, do you know what you are asking me to do? He is the top gunner's son.' I said there was no alternative, and Lascelles paused and said he would speak to Christison, the corps commander, with whom he had a good personal equation. Robin was moved within 24 hours to the field artillery training centre at Mathura. I was sorry to see him go, and we remained in touch till he passed away in 2008.

Robin was replaced by Lt John Willie Leckhe, a former planter from a tea garden in Assam. He was over 40 with scarcely any knowledge of gunnery. I tried to teach him, but to little avail, he insisting he was too old to learn! Leckhe spoke to our jawans as if they were labourers in his tea estate! I once reprimanded him about this and he retorted: 'Young man. I am old enough to be your father!'. He was really difficult to deal with. One day while moving along a jungle trail, I decided to recite a poem by Rudyard Kipling, but modified it for his benefit! (The original poem is *First Shikaris*). My version was:

A snider squibbled in the jungle,
Somebody laughed and fled,
And the men of 1 Battery picked up their subaltern dead,
With a blue mark on his forehead
And the back blown out of his head!

Leckhe, visibly shaken, screamed at me to stop. We proceeded along the trail on our mission without any further event. Later, I took up with headquarters the question of his replacement, and soon Leckhe was posted out to Movement Control in Cox's Bazaar.

After the jungles of Mayu range, the beach at Ukhia, stretching for miles down to Foul Point was indeed magnificent. We enjoyed the training there and were put on special rations including 'halal' New Zealand lamb. Our Punjabi Mussalman troops refused to accept the stamped 'halal' meat as authentic so we officers had more meat than we could consume. My knowledge of this beach was to prove useful later in the India-Pakistan war of 1971.

There was a vacancy for a battery commander in the regiment. The CO wrote to the brigade to post in a major as the British officers were not sufficiently fit and though Jacob was fit he was too junior. A British officer, Capt. Robinson proclaimed that if Jacob superseded him he would commit suicide. The brigade commander, who had seen me in action, responded with a one-liner: 'Jacob will be promoted.' Robinson came up to me in a belligerent mood, and I said: 'Robbie if you want to shoot yourself you are at liberty to do so,' and sulked off.

We were initially to assault the Andaman Islands, but the plan was later changed to capturing instead Ramree Island off the coast of Burma. Many years later, in 1960 at Fort Bragg, North Carolina, I attended a banquet given by the post commander, Brig. Gen. Richard G. Stillwell, son of 'Vinegar Joe' Stillwell (a US Army general best known for his service in China and Burma), with Lord Louis Mountbatten as the guest of honour. I was returning from a missile training course held at Fort Sill, Oklahoma, the training centre for the US army's artillery and was wearing my Indian army blue patrols. Mountbatten saw me and signalled me to sit beside him. We discussed the operations of the 26 Indian Division, particularly Ramree. Mountbatten said that initially the Andamans were chosen as our objective and the intelligence branch was told, as a deception cover plan, to simulate an attack on Ramree Island. The objective was later changed from the Andamans to Ramree. The intelligence, due to some mix up, was not informed and they continued to simulate an attack on Ramree.

My battery was to support the 1st battalion of the Lincolnshire Regiment, a British Army infantry battalion which formed part of an Indian Army infantry brigade, the other two infantry battalions being Indian, as was the norm up to and during the Second World War. Fortunately for us the intelligence had simulated the assault at Mount Peter which the Japanese had fortified, with tunnels and bunkers that had been dug deep into the hill. We landed at Kyakpau, further north, which was lightly held and the operations went according to plan. I was assigned as forward officer, bombardment, for the battleship HMS *Queen Elizabeth* of Britain's royal navy. I directed the fire of her eight 15-inch guns, firing 2000 lb shells at the Mount Peter defences. Later, when I went to see the results I was surprised how little damage had been inflicted on the bunkers. Over a 1000 soldiers of the Japanese garrison retreated into the crocodile-infested mangrove swamps. We went in with boats with interpreters using loud-hailers asking them to come out. Not a single one did. Salt-water crocodiles, some of them well over 20 ft in length frequented these waters. It is not difficult to imagine what happened to the Japanese who took refuge in the mangroves!

From Ramree we could watch the naval bombardment of Myebon. The British marines and commandos were bogged down. The 36th Indian Brigade of our division, commanded by Brigadier K.S. Thimayya, was ordered to clear out the Japanese, which they successfully did. Thimayya was the only Indian to command a brigade in battle during the Second World War. He was the most distinguished combat officer the Indian army has produced. With him was Lt Col S.P.P. Thorat and Lt Col L.P (Bogey) Sen. Lt Col Carriapa was at that time AQMG of the 26th Indian Division and Maj. Bikram Singh his deputy.

After clearing the Japanese out of Ramree, we took part in the landing at Letpan Chaung, south of Akyab, and also at Cheduba Island. The division was then promised a rest and refit back in India. We boarded a troopship, MV *Dunera*, and sailed to Madras; spirits were high as we were told we would be located near Bangalore. We docked in Madras in the late evening. The following morning we were awakened by announcements over loudspeakers to be ready to proceed on a route march in full field service marching order. There were grunts of outrage from the battalion of the Lincolnshire Regiment. It was raining heavily, and we marched through the streets of Madras cursing, wondering whether this was the recreation we had been promised. We returned to the ship late in the evening. The following morning we sailed out of Madras in stormy weather on very rough seas. There was intense speculation about where we were heading. Our doubts were soon removed when the shoreline of Ramree Island reappeared on the horizon. After anchoring, a motorboat pulled alongside. Maj. Gen. Chambers, who was earlier Brigadier, General Staff at HQ XV

Corps and promoted to replace our previous divisional commander, the popular Maj. Gen. Lomax, boarded the troopship. We were ordered to assemble on the deck to be addressed by Chambers. There was much fidgeting before Chambers began speaking. 'You should be very privileged to know that you have been asked to return here to take part in one of the most important strategic operations of the war, as for your leave …' was as far as he got. One of the soldiers of the Lincolns shouted 'Chums you've had it!!'. This was followed by catcalls and barracking. A red-faced Chambers descended to the motorboat alongside to continuing catcalls and barracking.

My battery returned to its previous location. There was nothing there. The shelters we had constructed from the tin sheets scrounged from the Japanese bunkers had disappeared, so we had to face another monsoon without cover. Soon a bevy of senior staff officers from various headquarters descended on us, including the supreme commander, Lord Louis Mountbatten. The division then prepared for the assault on Rangoon. The American Office of Strategic Services (OSS), Wild Bill Donovan's, boys whom we called the boat people, had informed us that the Japanese were pulling out of Rangoon. Despite this, the operation was executed as planned.

On the lighter side, I can recall one incident in particular when the German surrender was announced. The 6 Rajputana Rifles, whose task it was to protect the gun area, fired its mortars into the sea in celebration when I was in the gun area. Lt Col Hill, who was officiating as commander, Royal Artillery, of the Division, phoned and wanted to know who was firing. On being informed he ordered me to place the commanding officer, Lt Col Butcher, who I knew well, under arrest. The Officers' Mess was under a tarpaulin and there was revelry all around. I went up to Col Butcher and said, 'I have been sent to place you under arrest!'. He laughed and replied, 'Have a drink old boy,' and that was the end of the matter.

We returned to India after the fall of Rangoon by the same troopship and proceeded to a tented camp some 30 miles outside Bangalore and were told to prepare to take part in operation 'Zipper', the assault on Malaya.

I was asked to proceed to the selection board at Bangalore for a regular commission. The tests were exhaustive, tough, and spread over four days. Some weeks later my name was announced as one of the first to be given a regular commission.

Operation Zipper was never mounted. The first atom bomb was dropped on Hiroshima on 8 August and Japan surrendered shortly after. The division was to move to Sumatra to disarm the Japanese located there. The move was, however, delayed as General Douglas McArthur directed that moves would only take place after he signed the instrument of surrender aboard a battleship in Tokyo Bay. We embarked on troopships in Madras and sailed to the anchorage at Belawan in North Sumatra. There we collected our vehicles and equipment and proceeded to Medan. My battery was immediately involved in providing security for sensitive installations in the town. The Dutch officials were attempting to take over the government, a move that was strongly resisted by the Indonesians who wanted the Dutch to leave. Resistance was at first muted. 'Merdeka,' the cry for freedom, echoed throughout the archipelago. Fighting broke out between the Indonesians and our forces, which were given orders to return control of the country to the Dutch. The soldiers of my regiment were Punjabi Mussalman and their sympathy lay with the Indonesians. In those days artillery batteries were self-accounting units and were designed to operate independently. My battery was assigned the task of policing a large sector of the town, including a part of the perimeter. The Japanese unit located there presented me with a guard of honour. I remembered this when I was negotiating Niazi's surrender in 1971 and insisted on him providing a ceremonial guard of honour, for which he was much criticized.

I commandeered the Japanese commander's Packard convertible (previously owned by a Dutchman). It was a fabulous car in mint condition. I was not, however, destined to drive it around for very long. The general officer commanding the division, Maj. Gen. 'Deadly' Hedley saw me driving it and ordered that the car be handed over to him for his use, and that I would be given a suitable replacement. The replacement arrived, a beat-up Austin 10, which had seen better days. Hedley was later promoted to assume command in Malaya.

One of our soldiers disappeared somewhere in our sector and we organized a search operation. I was driving past a long double-storeyed wooden building and decided to have a look accompanied by my signal operator. The ground floor housed a cigar factory, humming with activity. In years gone by, the best cigars were wrapped in the famous Deli tobacco leaf of northern Sumatra. The workforce appeared to consist in the main of girls. They worked silently and all appeared peaceful. I was fascinated by the manner in which they rolled the cigars on their exposed thighs. We then decided to investigate the top floor. No sooner had we reached the top of the stairs, than we saw at the far end of the corridor a group of young 'Pemodas' armed with spears and they began hurling the latter at us. I fired over their heads, emptying a full magazine from my Luger pistol, to keep them at bay. My signaller, armed with a sten gun, ran down to cover me. The other signaller in the jeep also began firing at the top floor to cover our move to the jeep. I had been in battle before but had never been so unnerved as on this occasion, attacked by a fierce looking group of spear-throwing, machete-wielding freedom fighters!

The intelligence officer attached to our division was Captain Turco Westerling of the Dutch Army, a rough operator. The Indonesians had put a reward of US$20,000 in gold on his head. On a couple of occasions I had to admonish him for his methods. In one particular incident he tried to force his way across a bridge manned by my troops, to a 'no go ahead' area without a permit. The havildar in charge stopped him with the butt of his rifle.

Some weeks later a British service officer who had replaced Westerling, against my advice, accompanied by four British sergeants with a permit crossed over to the no-go area. Some days later the officer's body was dumped after nightfall on the far side of the bridge. Westerling used to boast that his Ambonese soldiers were superior to our Gurkhas. Later, after Indonesia became independent, he raised a revolt against the Indonesian government, using his favourite Ambonese troops. The revolt was crushed and Westerling returned to the Netherlands.

The Indonesians, despite the brutal Japanese occupation, preferred the Japanese to the Dutch. They refused to take Dutch guilders, accepting only the worthless Japanese currency. We regretted that on arrival we had burnt crates of the Japanese currency. The Japanese in defeat were disciplined and behaved with dignity. The working parties provided by them were a model of efficiency. Once assigned a task, they executed it silently and efficiently. We could only move out of Medan in battalion strength. I was deputed to carry out some assignments out of Medan and had to do so by travelling in the back of a Japanese truck, as the Indonesians did not interfere with the movement of Japanese troops. On one of my assignments out of Medan I had ordered a particular task to be carried out by the Japanese unit. I informed the commander that it had not been completed to my satisfaction. He called up the second in command, and, in front of his men, slapped him with his gloved hand. I was astounded and most impressed by the Japanese even in defeat.

On the various forays around Medan our columns were frequently ambushed by the Indonesians. On one occasion, moving with the 6th Battalion, Rajputana Rifles on the road to Arnhemia, the company commander walking beside me, Major Sabnis suggested that we separate as the road along which we were advancing was notorious for its frequent ambushes. He advised that I move to the other side of the road, which I did with my radio detachment. A few hundred yards ahead there was a burst of fire and Major Sabnis stopped four bullets, was evacuated, and survived the attack. In another operation, Major Chand was also seriously wounded.

3

Back to Deolali and Matters Relating to Partition

In mid-1946, I was selected with some eight others from the division, who had made a significant contribution to operations, to have a short holiday on the Island of Bali. We were flown out in a Dakota aircraft together with a jeep and trailer and landed on a grassy strip at Denpasar. The pilot told us he would be back in fourteen days. Bali was wonderful, unlike Sumatra, extremely peaceful, with no Japanese or Dutch troops on the island. We had the freedom to roam wherever we wanted. It seemed quite idyllic; there was no dress code as is now imposed. The women moved around topless. We attended the cultural performances and were enthralled by the dance troupes. I was fortunate to be invited by the famous Belgian artist Le Mayeur to be his guest at his beach bungalow at Denpasar. He had married his beautiful model Pollock. She was indeed, to say the least, stunning. We had barbecues on the beach accompanied by the local fiery arrack. I bought a water colour by Pollock from him. He insisted that the cheque be made out in straits dollars and not Dutch guilders. The portrait set in a carved Balinese wooden frame occupies pride of place in my bedroom. Two weeks of this paradise was all too brief.

The Dakota returned as scheduled. The Royal Air Force crew loaded a large number of pigs for their base. On our way back one of the engines failed. The captain of the aircraft asked us to jettison our baggage as we were losing height. We insisted that he first jettison the pigs. This they did over the sea, one by one. We managed to make it to an airfield at Palembang, where the engine was repaired. The Dakota was the workhorse of the air force, reliable, robust and readily repairable. There was nothing like it. They are still flying in many parts of the world. In November 1946, I was ordered to hand over my perimeter to the Dutch Army. This took place in an orderly manner and we disengaged. We were lined up to move to the anchorage at Belawan where troopships were waiting. Shortly after we had boarded our vehicles, the Indonesians began attacking the perimeter. The Dutch commandant ran up to me requesting we return. I expressed regrets as my orders were to reach Belawan at a specified time. We drove to Belawan and embarked for Madras.

I had been earmarked to attend one of the two courses: Allied Land Forces South East Asia had nominated me for the Air Observation Course and India Command had detailed me to attend the Gunnery Staff Course, designed to train instructors in gunnery. I opted for the Gunnery Staff Course and embarked on a crowded troopship for Glasgow, Scotland. Conditions on board and amenities were very basic. We arrived at Glasgow in a snowstorm. We tried to get something to eat at a restaurant in Saucihall street. Rationing was in force and we had to make do with a stew of offal and Brussel sprouts. We took the train to London, and the unheated train was held up en route by snow drifts. We eventually reached the Artillery School at Larkhill in a very cold winter; one of the coldest in living memory. There were shortages of almost everything. Our quarters in the mess were unheated. We were, however, provided with girls of the ATS rather than male batmen. I had since 1942 served in the Middle East, Burma, and Sumatra under difficult conditions, and was hoping for some relaxation and fun. I did not exert much effort to study and went out to London most weekends. I was to regret this attitude later when on my return to India I was assigned to teach the same course I had attended here.

During the Easter break I went to Torquay on the coast in southern England and stayed at the Osborne, a lovely old-fashioned hotel with large ornate suites. There were some pretty girls there chaperoned by their doting mothers. Dances were organized every evening with an old-fashioned band in attendance. I was to catch the train on the night of Easter Monday but was persuaded by my dancing partner who was from the area of Amesbury, close to Larkhil, to dance on till late into the night. My partner promised that she and her mother would drive me back early in the morning. I foolishly agreed. Early next morning I tried to wake them up in the hotel but with no success. Later that morning we drove to Larkhill. In those days the classrooms were housed in hutted accommodation. We reached after lunch and the instructor, Major 'Fatty' Price was standing outside. He took one look at the occupants of the car, and a broad smile spread across his face. I mumbled, 'I can explain', but before I could cook up some cock and bull story, he said, 'There is no need to explain', and handed me a question paper for the examination in progress. After that, he would good humouredly refer to me as 'Lord Jacob of Torquay'. Many years later when I was commandant of the Artillery School, two officers were marched up before me for a somewhat similar lapse. The chief instructor demanded their scalps. I gave them a sharp dressing down and told them not to repeat it. An agitated chief instructor could not understand why I had not punished them as he had recommended. I explained that I had committed a similar lapse and was not penalized and therefore considered that it would be highly unfair in the circumstances for me to punish them.

On completion of the course, Major Apte, a course-mate, and I decided to hire a chauffeur-driven car and went off to fish for salmon near the delightful little village of Killin on the western end of Loch Tay in Scotland. Before returning to India we spent a fortnight in Paris. Prices were still reasonable, and I recall Maxims, Fouquets, Lido, and the now defunct Bal Tabarin. We visited the museums, Napoleon's tomb at Versailles, and Fountainbleau.

I boarded an Anchor line ship for Bombay in early August 1947 scheduled to arrive in Bombay on 17 August to an independent India and Pakistan. There were many officers on board who were destined to serve in the armed forces of both the countries. There was still a spirit of comraderie aboard when we disembarked at Bombay.

The train chugged up the Western Ghats through verdant forests and then past Lake Beale. The familiar panorama of Deolali emerged, conical hill, Bahula Fort, and Siva Donga. The railway station looked just the same. I got into a tonga and got off at the mess and was allotted a quarter on Connaught road. This was, however, a different Deolali to that I had left in 1942. Partition had created an atmosphere of tension. Besides, Deolali had become a major transit centre for British troops and their families returning to Great Britain. A very large camp, Homeward Bound Trooping Depot, had been set up for families awaiting a passage back to Britain.

I reported to the commandant, Brig. 'Fatty' Frowen. Frowen had lost a leg in the western desert and was as a result taken prisoner, though later freed by advancing British troops. General Montgomery, visiting released prisoners of war, rebuked him for allowing himself to be captured. Frowen's reply was classic: 'Sir, you too would have been taken prisoner had you left a leg behind!' Montgomery, taken aback, did not reply and moved on. Frowen briefed me on the splitting of the school resources between India and Pakistan and as the senior Indian officer, the other being my friend Major 'Bhayya' Apte, I was to be responsible for taking over the assets of the school and overseeing the division of resources of the establishment between India and Pakistan.

Two courses were to commence in August 1947; the gunnery staff course designed to train instructors in gunnery and the young officers' course. I was to take the gunnery course and Apte that for young officers. I reported to the chief instructor, gunnery, a British officer who, on his way out. He was completely disinterested, his office in apparent disarray. He handed me an outline syllabus based on the old superseded gunnery methods. I told him that the gunnery methods had changed and that I had brought with me drafts of the new techniques. He said that the gunnery wing was using gunnery doctrines established during the Second World War and as far as he was concerned I should teach them. I retorted that this was a retrograde step and that I would see the commandant. The commandant, when briefed, agreed with me and spoke to the chief instructor. Frowen was to leave in a few weeks.

I liked Frowen. Though he only had one active leg (the other artificial) he played tennis regularly, and I partnered him on several occasions. He was indeed a distinguished individual.

On the course I was to take, there were several officers waiting to return to Pakistan; their move back was delayed up to November. There were isolated communal killings in the area. Three bodies were found dumped in the nullah some yards from our quarters. Some officers who were to go to Pakistan asked me if they could move into my quarters for some time, moving out some days later because no further incidents occurred.

I was kept very busy teaching as well as performing other allotted tasks. I had perforce to take all the classes, and supervising the division of the assets of the school between India and Pakistan was exasperating. Moreover, I had to ensure that the assets of the Temple Hill club were not frittered away by the demands of returning British officers for consumption of the food and wine stocks at heavily discounted prices. By early 1948, a few more instructors arrived after training at Larkhill. Lt Col Sartaj Singh, Major O.P. Malhotra, Major Reggie Prasad, Major Ralph Foregard, among others, joined the staff. The course I was teaching passed out in March 1948, largely making up for the shortages of instructors at the school.

We bachelors in the mess had a great deal of fun off duty hours. There were dances at the club and no shortage of partners, as many of the British girls bound for 'Blighty' wanted to stay back in India. Luckily I managed, despite temptations, to remain single. Later, when most of the British returned, we would, on many a Saturday night, catch a train to Igatpuri. Igatpuri had a large Anglo-Indian population and the dances organized at the railway institute were lively. We changed into our dinner jackets in the waiting room at the railway station to conform to the dress code. Sometimes there were problems with the protective and aggressive attitude of male escorts. John Masters, in his novel *Bhowani Junction,* describes their outlook and inhibitions. Masters who had served with the Gurkhas in the regular army before, and for a short time after Independence, used Jhansi as the locale for his novel, but could equally well have used Igatpuri. I spent three wonderful years at Deolali as an instructor and had to travel a great deal all over India to calibrate the guns of our regiments because the other instructors who had returned from Larkhill had their course truncated, missing the instruction on calibration.

My next assignment in 1950 was at Army Headquarters, Directorate of Artillery, as a general staff officer grade II, a major's appointment. The artillery was in the process of reorganization, I heading the section on equipment and training. We had to revise the establishments of units and equipment schedules. Brig. P.S. Gyani was the director, a soft-spoken officer. He occasionally called me for briefings which were long and rambling. I was at a loss trying to figure out what he was driving at. Gyani was soon replaced by Brig. P.P. Kumaramangalam. 'K', as he was affectionately known, was outgoing and personable with a somewhat mischievous sense of humour. We got on extremely well and developed a relationship of mutual trust and respect, and this continued throughout his service and well after. 'K' was taken prisoner in the Western Desert after the battle of Bir Hachiem, was awarded the DSO for his gallantry in action, and later freed by advancing British troops. He was married to a charming Parsi lady. 'K' trusted me and gave me a free hand. I worked closely with Brig. C.T. Edward Collins, an officer of the armoured corps, who headed the weapons and equipment directorate. We had to standardize the policy in relation to various items of equipment, so he asked me to write the policy on production of propellants for the three services. I had to make a choice between Picrites and the W group of propellants, the latter being favoured by the armoured corps and navy. I chose the Picrite group, a decision which stood the test of time. There were many other decisions I took, and in the process struck up a friendship with the scientific adviser, Dr Kothari. He was a kind and generous man who always responded to my requests for clarification of problems. I also sought advice from Lt Col Stan Doig who was at the Electrical and Mechanical Directorate. His younger brother Desmond had been a classmate of mine at school. Stan was artistically minded and introduced me to amateur dramatics in Delhi.

I applied to sit for the entrance exam for the Defence Services Staff College, requesting Brig. 'K' for a fortnight's leave to study. 'K' retorted that as I had already done a gunnery staff course there was no need for me to go to staff college, and in the event of my appearing for the examination, he would not nominate me. In those days the first few in ranking in the examination were entitled to a competitive vacancy. I responded that I did not require his nomination and that I would get a competitive vacancy. 'K' laughed good-humouredly, saying, 'Go ahead, I wish you luck'. I passed out top.

We had an enjoyable time in Delhi. We were billeted in Queen Victoria Road Officers' Mess, which was the home of bachelor officers of the army and navy. Lutyens Delhi was in those days a delightful uncrowded place. We not only worked hard but were able to enjoy recreational facilities at the gymkhana and defence club. We played tennis, squash, and golf at the Delhi Golf Club. Membership of these clubs was exclusive and restricted to the services and top Indian administrative service officers. Brig 'K', whenever he came to Delhi from Deolali, stayed in my room and I moved into that of a friend. No car was in those days provided nor accommodation. I placed my car at his disposal.

I had to join the course at the Staff College. I bade farewell to Brig 'K'. It was indeed a pleasure to have served on his staff. He stood by me when the Master General of Ordnance, Lt Gen. Sant Singh demanded my scalp for signing policy letters which he considered to be his prerogative. He objected to my finalizing the uniforms of the Regiment of Artillery without his approval, as also other policy letters on propellants and *fuzes* for the three services. He ordered us to change the motto of the regiment 'Izzat o Iqbal' because it was in roman Urdu and to replace it with a Hindi one. I explained that there was no equivalent for *izzat*. We stuck it out and managed to retain our motto.

4

At Staff College and the Years that Followed

The Defence Services Staff College was located at Wellington in the Nilgiri hills in south India. We took the narrow gauge mountain railway train to Wellington station, winding through the lovely countryside, past coconut and areca-nut plantations and manicured tea bushes. The commandant, Maj. Gen. Joe Lentaigne had as a brigadier served under Maj. Gen. Orde Wingate during the Chindit operations in Burma, assuming command of the force after Wingate was killed in an air crash. He did not get on with Wingate whom he considered to be a poseur and charlatan. He also disliked General 'Vinegar' Joe Stillwell with whom he had serious differences on the conduct of operations in north Burma, and considered him to be a narrow-minded Anglophobe with tunnel vision, unable to grasp the overall strategic priorities.

The initiative for setting up an inter-Services Staff College for the army, navy, and air force was taken by Lord Louis Mountbatten, who had earlier, during the Second World War, been largely responsible for the initial impetus for combined operations. The groundwork and establishment of this institution was the work of Joe Lentaigne. The Staff College is today internationally recognized as one of the premier institutions of its kind. Much of the credit for this should go to Lentaigne.

I remember his human side. I was having problems with one of the instructors from the Army Service Corps who wrote a long-winded critique in red ink on a thesis I had written, with a final comment 'waffle' which he underlined. This instructor had never taken part in any operation, serving in non-combat zones. I wrote 'waffle' against his long-winded comments and forgot about it. Sometime later he called for our papers to put the best and worst to the commandant. He was furious to see my comment on his note, and sent it to the commandant. I was told that the commandant wished to see me. Lentaigne had gone through the relevant papers and removed his reading glasses and looked me up and down. I was expecting a severe dressing down, but was taken aback when he said, 'Jacob, you must learn to suffer fools'. Joe Lentaigne took a liking to me and would often discuss the Chindit operations in Burma with me. He was a soldier of the old school, and I learnt much from him.

I made many friends at the Staff College. This was to stand me in good stead in later years. I was originally assigned as brigade major of an infantry brigade, but this was changed to command of 75 Patiala Mountain Battery. I was instructed to report to Brig. Kumaramangalam (K) at Delhi before assuming command. Brig K briefed me on why he was sending me to command the battery. Patiala Mountain Battery had been part of Patiala State Forces and was merged with the Indian Army after Independence. 'K' told me that the men had shot and killed a junior commissioned officer and the battery havildar (sergeant) major, and that I should sort out the battery. The battery was spread out from Udhampur, where there was a rear detachment, to Tangdhar, a distance of several hundred miles, and its guns were deployed in two locations. A troop of 25 pounder field guns was put under my command. A mountain battery was one of the finest commands a major could hope for, and designated the '*Corps de elite*' of the gunners. Earlier, in 1950, at Army HQ, I had designed a special lanyard for the mountain artillery, and this was later authorized for all ranks of the artillery. Today this lanyard has been hijacked by various police formations and, sadly, by personnel of private security agencies. I had worked with mountain batteries in Burma and was impressed by their elan. A mountain battery was manned by four officers, three junior commissioned officers, and

275 men. A signal section with a veterinary officer and regimental medical officer were also assigned together with 96 mules and 25 chargers. I had since my childhood loved horses and, as a boy in Calcutta, used to exercise race horses at a local stable. I soon got to love the mules too. The mountain artillery mules were specially bred as they had to carry heavy loads; very few of them could carry the cradle, a top load. Life in a mountain battery was hard; terribly hard. Mules and horses required constant attention, with regular feeding and grooming. Mules, I found, were far more intelligent than horses. Over rough terrain a mule, unlike a horse, would feel and prod its way to check whether the going was safe. Initially, mountain artillery gun mules were obtained from Missouri in the US and later from South Africa.

Tangdhar in the Kashmir Valley was on the far side of the Nastachun Pass, at a height of over 10,000 ft. Given the heavy winter snows, the dirt road winding through the pass is closed for six months. Avalanches were frequent and therefore crossing the pass to stock provisions for the winter was quite an adventure. Our battery had to provide fire support over a very large area, from Nastachun Pass, Tutmari *gali* right down to Kishenganga river. The *deodar* (cedar) forest ridges were lovely. I enjoyed visiting the numerous piquets spread along the mountain ridges.

The class composition of the battery was Sikh, Jat, and Lobana. Initially, I found them somewhat difficult to handle but I was soon able to gain their confidence, trust, and respect. They were tough and dependable, and excellent gunners.

In the summer of 1952, the battery was ordered to move to Poonch via Jammu, several hundred-road miles away, a very long march. We covered some 20 miles a day. It was a difficult routine: up early morning, water and feed the horses and mules, saddle up, load and march to the next camping ground. Our advance party in vehicles would set up camp and prepare the evening meal. On arrival, the animals were watered, fed, and groomed; only after that could the men have their meal. This went on day after day until we reached Poonch some three weeks later. As the men marched I forbade officers to ride, remembering how we as cadets had cursed our company commander for sitting smugly astride his charger.

Poonch was the scene of heavy fighting in 1948. Poonch was known for its fort and palace, and we camped in a delightful garden, Rani Bagh. The fort was a semi ruin, and we were given charge of it for use as an ammunition dump. The battery's operational responsibility was spread over a very large area. The brigade commander, Brig. Rawat was commissioned in Jammu & Kashmir State Forces. He was physically tough and energetic, and we used to visit all the defence locations atop the ridges. I learnt a great deal from him. One of the things he drove home was that in mountain warfare counter-attacks were extremely difficult to mount and therefore a better alternative was to reinforce the position under attack. Rawat was replaced by a brigadier from the Army Service Corps. I was sorry to see him go.

The divisional commander was scheduled to visit. He liked to see his photograph prominently displayed. There was only one photograph of his in the brigade. After each visit to a unit, a dispatch rider would in turn transport the photograph to the next unit to be visited. The general was also fond of inspecting the unit quarter guard. We had a problem; we only had one trumpeter and he was on leave. The infantry units used the bugle. The general was entitled to a general salute before inspecting the quarter guard. The previous evening I went round the lines asking if anyone could sound the trumpet calls. One old mule leader said he could sound the 'stables' call but not the general's salute. The calls on the bugle and trumpet are different. I told the soldier to play the stables call, confident that the general would not know the difference. The inspection went off well, the general leaving in a good mood. That night I was asked to the brigade mess for dinner and after dinner bridge. The brigade commander normally partnered the general, and he advised me that the general liked to win. I replied that I too liked to win. The general lost a modest sum and gruffly told me that his aide-de-camp would settle later. I replied that it was customary to settle wins and losses at the table. He frowned, took out his wallet, and settled. I was never again invited to play bridge at the brigade officers' mess.

The battery was camping outside Poonch when we were visited by the brigadier, Artillery of HQ Western Command, Brig. Anup Singh Kalha. I had met him during the Second World War when he was a captain and I a major. Later, when sent to report on one of his units, he shouted at me 'Jacob, are you commanding this unit or I?' I responded, 'Brigadier, neither you nor I are commanding this unit, the commanding officer is standing there', pointing to him. The brigadier arrived at our tented mess for dinner. He made numerous demands for a variety of things. He then tasted the soup and said, 'Jacob this is barley soup!', implying that I was serving him barley from the mule rations. I replied that if he did not like his soup he need not have it. Other unpleasant exchanges followed. I could take it no more and said, 'Brigadier, kindly leave this mess'. He then shouted, 'You will parade your battery, mules, guns ready for war for my inspection at 0600 hours tomorrow morning!'. I replied that I would do no such thing as he was only a staff officer and had no authority to issue such orders. I asked 2/Lt Satnam Singh (retd Lt Gen.) to escort him to his jeep. He visited the unit in the morning and found fault with everything he saw. I kept my cool. Before he left he asked me for a packed lunch. As he had commented nastily on our mess food, I told the senior JCO to put some vegetable curry and four chappatis from the men's cookhouse wrapped in newspaper in his jeep. Some time later division HQ sent me a copy of his technical report for me to comment on. It read as follows: 'This officer is well below average. He has no knowledge of gunnery or administration. He has to be spoon-fed', and so it went on and on. A full page of negative comments! I had done a gunnery staff course in the UK and had taught gunnery at the School of Artillery for three years and was a graduate of the Defence Services Staff College (Anup Singh had no qualifications whatsoever). I sent my reply: 'Brig Anup Singh is entitled to his opinions.' Many years later, in 1957, when he was sub-area commander in Ambala, there was an enquiry being conducted against him. I invited him to my mess. He asked me, 'Jacob, why do people not like me?' I replied, 'Why should they; what good have you done that they should like you?'. He said, 'Jacob, you don't understand. When I was in 1 Field Regiment as a captain, one day on the ranges I was at the OP, Captain Summanwar was at the gun position. Summanwar fired a wrong round. My British commanding officer Horsfield fixed me. After that anyone who reminded me of Horsfield I fixed.' I responded, 'So many officers must have reminded you of Horsfield'. He retired shortly thereafter.

From Poonch the battery moved to Rajouri. We camped near the grassy airstrip below the old fort. Here we were able to get the most out of our horses. We practised handy hunter jumping and show jumping, and used the airstrip to race. Some time later I was taken aback to receive a bill from the military engineering services amounting to several thousand rupees for damages alleged to have been caused to the airstrip by the hooves of our horses. This was disputed by us and ignored. No penalty was paid.

I had completed two years in command of the mountain battery and was expecting to go as brigade major of an infantry brigade but was surprised to receive a phone call from Brig. Kumaramangalam, the Director of Artillery, that he was sending me, at the request of Brig. K.P. Candeth, the commander of 1st Artillery Brigade of 1st Armoured Division, as his brigade major. Apparently the performance of the brigade during recent manoeuvres had come in for a great deal of adverse criticism. I reported to 1st Armoured Artillery Brigade at Jullundur. The division moved shortly after to Jhansi. It was early 1954. The move of our brigade headquarters was enjoyable. We had opportunities en route to shoot partridge, sand grouse, and duck for the pot. Jhansi was to become the home of the armoured division.

Jhansi cantonment was established by the British after the Mutiny of 1857. Jhansi Fort, a most impressive and formidable structure, was famous for its association with the gallant Rani of Jhansi, one of India's most revered freedom fighters, who was killed in battle. Her body was later found dressed as a soldier. The Rani has a special place in Indian history, and is indeed a legend. Big game hunting was legally licenced then. I shot a tiger and several leopards, the latter at the request of the villagers as these leopards were preying on their goats. On one such trip I came across a leopard cub apparently lost. I looked around for the mother with no success. I got permission from the authorities to rear the cub and named her Sabrina.

I was fortunate to have bought a custom-built MG four-seater sports car which had been earlier owned by a former ruler of a small princely state. It was a pleasure to drive and had a light aluminium body and independent jacking controlled from the cab. The commander, artillery brigade, Brig. K.P. Candeth was a soldier of the old school. We got on well, remained in close touch, and our friendship lasted throughout his life. His death some years ago naturally saddened me. I was indeed fortunate in having a close rapport with both Candeth and Kumaramanglam, both officers with great love for the Regiment of Artillery.

I had got an out-of-turn promotion to major in Burma. After Independence, promotions were governed by the date of one's commission. Fortunately for me the government decided to raise more artillery regiments, and after a tenure of 11 years as a major, I was promoted in May 1956 to the rank of Lt Colonel and assigned to raise the 3rd Field Regiment in Delhi Cantonment. I drove to Delhi from Jhansi with Sabrina, my leopard, sitting beside me. On reporting to the area commander, I requested that some accommodation be provided to enable me to commence raising the regiment, for which officers and men were beginning to arrive. I requested the area commander to allot me some barracks. His attitude was far from friendly. He told me that my regiment was not one of the units that was on his order of battle, and he was not therefore in a position to allot any accommodation. I knew the commanding officer of 19 Heavy Anti-aircraft Regiment and requested him to help out. He most generously loaned two of his barracks.

We commenced raising. After a few weeks, the infantry battalion located in makeshift lines on the northern outskirts of the city at Anand Parbat was ordered to move out. I requested the general, Maj. Gen. V.C. Dubey, to allot to me these lines that were to be vacated. After much discussion he reluctantly agreed with the proviso that I would vacate the lines as and when required by him. I readily agreed, aware that 'possession is nine-tenths of the law'. I had known Maj. Gen. Dubey earlier when my mountain battery was part of his division and was destined to serve as his principal general staff officer again two years later.

Raising a regiment from scratch is hard work. We had to create the infrastructure as well as weld the officers and men into a viable entity. Fortunately there was an artillery range at Tuglakabad nearby. We were able to carry out live firing practices with our dependable 25-pounder guns. The 25 pounder developed prior to the Second World War was the standard equipment of the field artillery and was used extensively in almost all theatres of operations. It continued in service into the 1980s and served as the artillery's work-horse. We were all saddened to see it phased out. After some six months the regiment was exercised both tactically and technically, and declared 'fit for war'. During this camp, the residents of a village near Qutub Minar asked me to shoot a leopard which was carrying away goats from the village. I examined the pugmarks on the outskirts of the village and arrived there just before sunset and took up position amongst some bushes a little distance from the pugmarks. It was getting dark. After half an hour I noticed a slight movement in the bushes a few yards ahead and fired. The leopard leapt at me, but fortunately I was able to fire another round to stop him. The villagers were delighted and thanked me profusely. I sent the skin to the famous taxidermists Van Ingen and Van Ingen in Mysore. This mounted skin was presented later to the Artillery School, Deolali.

The unit was raised from Static Post Groups (small artillery sub-units) in Jammu & Kashmir. The Post Groups were manned by the throwouts from all units. I went to see a colleague and requested him to issue an amendment to the letter of raising. I told him that no one would discover it. The amendment read 'for all India read Sikh', and was issued. 3rd Field became an all Sikh Regiment and there was no fallout.

The regiment was visited by Maj. Gen. B.K. (Biji) Kaul, an officer of the Army Service Corps, who had cultivated and impressed the defence minister, V.K. Krishna Menon. Kaul claimed to be related to Prime Minister Nehru. He informed me that he was asking for my regiment to be allotted to his division as, according to him, he had heard that I was a competent officer. We moved to Ambala where Kaul's 4 Infantry Division was located. The division had an outstanding record during the Second World War in the Middle East and Burma and was one of the crack divisions of the army.

We moved into barracks that were originally constructed as stables, without electricity and other standard amenities. The division was to be exercised by the command headquarters. Kaul, whose knowledge of operations at divisional level was minimal, called me for preliminary discussions on the handling of the division in the manoeuvres that were being organized to test the division. Shortly after, a Chinese military delegation was to visit. Kaul ordered me to organize a firepower demonstration of the divisional artillery. During the banquet organized for the visitors I was taken aback by the remarks of a Chinese general that 'China would never forget that Indian troops took part in the sacking and looting of the Summer Palace during the 2nd Opium war'. He went on to make other contentious remarks. This was in 1958 when the slogan being bandied about by politicians was '*Hindi-Chini Bhai Bhai*' (Indians and Chinese are brothers). I reported the conversation but was told by Kaul that I must have misunderstood the Chinese general. I replied that I had not. Kaul did little to conceal his resentment. There were other signals of Chinese hostility, but these too were brushed aside by the politicians. Kaul was to be later humiliated and forced to retire after his incompetent and disastrous planning, first as chief of the general staff, and later in command of the combat forces that were ordered by Jawaharlal Nehru and Krishna Menon to evict the Chinese. Interestingly, during the Second World War, Kaul worked with an organization that provided entertainment for Indian troops in the war zone.

Kaul was a political general, militarily incompetent and over-ambitious. He used his political connections to bypass his seniors and influence policy. I recall one particular occasion when he invited Lt Col Eric Vas, an infantry battalion commander, and me for tea. We were stunned by the proposal he made to us, namely, that he was selecting officers of talent to form part of a core group he was recruiting. We fidgeted, trying first to figure out what he was driving at and how to respond. We had earlier heard of some talk about this special group. I looked at Vas, who winked knowingly. I then replied, 'Sir, as officers of your division, it is our bounden duty to further the interests of the division and army'. He snapped back, 'You damn well know what I mean; I want your total commitment to me.' Both Vas and I managed to beat a hasty retreat, leaving untouched the sumptuous tea laid out!

The division was very short of married accommodation, funds for building being scarce. Kaul told Krishna Menon that he would build the accommodation at minimum cost using troop labour. I objected to Kaul's demands, saying that my unit was a newly raised one and that I required time for training and, as such, we could not provide manpower for his building projects. Other confrontations took place and there was much tension. Kaul hit back at the regiment by instructing his military police to book our gunners for alleged violations. I was most unhappy and at one point considering resigning. Gen. Kumaramanglam heard about this and as my minimum tenure as a commanding officer was about to be completed, he had me assigned to take over as general staff officer grade (GSO) 1 of HQ Delhi and Rajasthan area.

The Delhi and Rajasthan area comprised of the whole of Rajasthan and the Union Territory of Delhi, the seat of the government of India. The area was responsible for the defence of the complete border with Pakistan from Barmer in the south to the Punjab. To carry out its task it was allotted a variety of troops, ranging from infantry brigades, armoured regiments, field artillery, and anti-aircraft regiments, camel-mounted infantry, and a horse-cavalry regiment. The central government in Delhi made numerous demands, calling out the army to assist with floods, running the water supply, and providing manpower for tasks which were not of a military nature. We were even required to provide horses and soldiers for the film *Mughal-e-Azam*.

The area was commanded by Maj. Gen. U.C. Dubey as GSO 1. I was responsible for operations and training. Another Lt Col was responsible for administration. Today, the Delhi area consists only of the Union Territory of Delhi, but the staff is several times as large as that of the former Delhi and Rajasthan area.

This assignment was productive and enjoyable. We set exercises for troops spread throughout Rajasthan. The UNCTAD conference was scheduled to be held in Delhi and there were reports that Delhi's water supply was contaminated. The prime minister was most concerned and directed that the army take control of the water supply. The defence minister summoned me to his office as the general was not contactable.

Krishna Menon then ordered the army to operate and maintain the Delhi water supply. When I protested that I knew nothing about water supply, Menon sarcastically retorted that I could learn. Brig. Noshir B. Grant of the Engineers and I visited the site at Wazirabad. Grant found that the intake for the water supply on the river Yamuna was some 50 yards upstream of a sewage outlet. The problem was soon solved by constructing a baffle wall separating the intake and outlet. Menon insisted on daily quality reports on the purity of the water. The task was time-consuming, so we made a representation that as the water supply had returned to normal, it should be handed back to the civic authorities. Menon did not agree. Some six months later Krishna Menon, accompanied by Gen. Thimayya, was visiting us to witness a demonstration. I told Menon that as the water supply was back to normal, its operation should be handed back to the authorities concerned. There was no reply. I repeated the request for a second and third time. Menon turned back, looked me up and down and remarked in his usual sarcastic manner, 'Colonel, I heard you the first time'. A few days later we were ordered to hand back the water supply to the authorities concerned.

A team from the Armalite factory in the US was in Delhi to promote their light-weight 5.56 mm weapons system. I was ordered to carry out the trials in Delhi and found it a very good weapon system. After comprehensive and exhaustive trials we recommended it for introduction. The system had not yet been bought by any country and the Armalite team indicated that they would consider participating in joint production in India. I was shocked at the response from the infantry directorate, opining that the rifle was unsuitable because it did not meet one of the general staff's requirements, of firing a four-inch group at 100 yards, the weapon firing a six inch group. More amazingly, they eventually rejected the rifle because it was unsuitable for ceremonial drill. This weapon system was later adopted by the American armed forces (M 16) and several other armies. The Indian Army opted to manufacture a virtual copy of the heavier Belgian FN rifle, which was more suitable for ceremonial drill. After some thirty years the Indian ordnance factories produced its version of the Armalite, the 5.56 mm INSAS rifle. This rifle is yet to overcome all its teething troubles and it will be years before all units are equipped with it.

Krishna Menon did little to conceal his dislike for the US, refusing to consider purchasing the proven Lockheed C130, opting instead for the British Avro 748. The Avro 748 is being phased out and the C130 is now been inducted into service. Krishna Menon's tenure as defence minister was to prove a disaster for the armed forces. He did little to modernize their weapons and equipment and attempted to politiclize the forces by promoting and placing in key positions some politically motivated officers of dubious capability. Gen. Thimayya objected to this policy and put in his resignation. His military assistant, Lt Col S.Y. Munshi was a colleague and friend. I often used to visit him at Army House, the residence of the Chief of Army Staff and sometimes the chief used to call him for discussions. I knew Thimayya from our meetings in the Arakan with my previous commanding officer, John Daniells, the commander, Royal Artillery and officiating commander of 25 Infantry Division. Munshi used to ask me to accompany him whenever I was there. Later, at one such meeting, Thimayya seemed agitated and perturbed. He had put in his papers due to the unwarranted interference and cavalier behaviour of Krishna Menon. He said that Prime Minister Nehru had called him and requested him to take back his resignation. Munshi advised him against withdrawal. Thimayya then said that Nehru had pleaded with him, saying that his resignation would cause a crisis in the country, and that in the national interest he should withdraw his resignation. Thimayya unfortunately took back his resignation. Later in parliament Nehru chided Thimayya, accusing him of being impetuous for one day resigning and on the following day taking back his resignation. Such is the world of politics. Thereafter, Thimayya was a 'lame duck'. Army chief K.K. Thimayya was the most brilliant combat officer the army had produced and had distinguished himself by commanding a brigade in operations in the Arakan. Later, during operations in Jammu & Kashmir, it was his 'guts' and audacious and systematic clearing of Zojila that saved Ladakh. He was a soldiers' soldier unlike some of the political, public relations-oriented army chiefs, bending backwards to accede to the whims and fancies of their political masters.

I was detailed to attend the Advanced Artillery and Missile course at Fort Sill, Oklahama and Fort Bliss, Texas in the US. I was surprised to be summoned by Defence Minister Krishna Menon for a briefing. It was indeed exceptional for the minister to interview officers prior to attending a foreign course. He embarked upon a long tirade against the US, pausing only to offer me a cup of tea and some biscuits. Krishna Menon's staff, on his frequent visits to the cantonment, insisted that the minister be served English biscuits with his tea, of which he drank numerous cups throughout the day.

We had to go to a lot of trouble to find English biscuits. I picked up the biscuit expecting to see an English brand but it proved to be a perfectly good Indian one!

Menon saw the smirk on my face and gave me a filthy look. He continued with his tirade. I then asked him why, if he indeed felt that way about the US, was he sending me to do a course of instruction there. Another tirade followed. He then told me to leave. I saluted and left post-haste. It was most unfortunate for India that Krishna Menon was appointed defence minister. His left-wing political leanings were well known; he was ambitious, and attempted to politiclize the armed forces, placing his personal appointees in key positions. The military disasters of 1962 are almost entirely due to his pro-leftist assessments that China would never attack India. He was a champion of '*Hindi-Chini Bhai Bhai*' (Indians and Chinese are brothers). His lack of any military expertise pushed us into a conflict for which, given his negligence, we were not equipped to fight. History has been too kind to him, and he was, in my view, by far the guiltiest individual for the 1962 debacle!

I was sorry to leave Delhi cantonment where I had been allotted a large bungalow with a rambling garden. I was considering getting married to a very lovely girl from Gujarat. She was in the National Cadet Corps (NCC) and a college professor. We dated for some three months. She then arranged for me to meet her father, and he approved of the marriage. Then came the bombshell! She told me that she was the only bread-winner in her family and that we would have to support her mother, father, and three school-going sisters! I explained that my meagre army pay would be insufficient for this. She cried but I stood my ground. I was extremely sorry that I had to end the affair. Many are the times I think of her.

My move to the US as well as some other circumstances brought the affair to an abrupt end, and I left for the US distraught. Passing through Bombay at the embarkation headquarters I ran into Gen. Kaul who now held a key appointment in army headquarters. He was surprised to see me, indicating that he was unaware of my assignment. I told him that if he so wished he could have my assignment cancelled as I was not all keen to go on another course of instruction. He did not answer, grunted, and strode away.

5

Training in the US and Back

I fitted in very well in the US as I had previous contacts with the army there during the Second World War. The course commenced in September 1959. I bought a used 1955 Ford for $400 and drove from Fort Sill to Fort Bliss, Texas near El Paso for the air defence leg of the course. The school at Fort Bliss was commanded by Brig. Gen. Mellnick who had earlier been a prisoner of war of the Japanese. I had earlier thought that the Americans were not very protocol conscious and was therefore taken aback to witness the entry of the one star general to the officers' club. His ADC preceded him carrying a pennant with one star, and this was placed on the dinner table. Then the brigadier general accompanied by his wife sat down.

The air defence missile systems were new to me and I had to work hard to keep pace with the rest. The adjacent well laid out town of EI Paso was a lively place. We often used to cross the bridge over the Rio Grande to Juarez, Mexico, which features in one of Graham Greene's short stories. After completing the course, I drove back to Fort Sill and was allotted a small room in a temporary barrack. This was not too much of a problem. I did not mind showering with others as I was used to this from my school days, though I found it difficult to stomach squatting in the company of others to relieve myself. I asked for a quarter with a more private toilet facility, a request that was not acceded to. Officers from Asian countries were housed in these quarters, while those from the US and NATO countries were provided with proper accommodation. Furthermore, as I was an officer of the rank of Lt Col, I resented receiving notes to go and tidy my room. I rented a small house in Lawton and moved out of the post. This was not well received by the commandant. The officers attending the course, some 400 in number, captains and majors, were from the regular army, US Marine Corps, and ROTC (Reserve Officers Training Corps) with me as the solitary Lt Colonel attending the course. I had seen combat in Burma and Sumatra, had qualified in the gunnery staff course in the UK, taught at the School of Artillery in India, and graduated from our Defence Services Staff college. Some of the instructors with limited credentials were uneasy at my presence. I found the marine corps officers a cut or two above the rest. I got on well with the South Koreans, Philippinos, and Vietnamese on the course. The American officers did not treat their Vietnamese colleagues with much respect. When I asked them why, I was shocked by the reply, 'Why should we treat them any better; they were our house-boys in Vietnam'. I had lived under British imperialism in India and had served in the British Indian Army but had never encountered such remarks before. This was the era when Little Rock had gained notoriety for the intermittent violence between blacks and whites, a major episode occurring in 1958. I did little to conceal my feelings. This did not go down well with the establishment. This was also the McCarthyist era. One of my colleagues on the course confided in me that he had been asked to report on his brother officers. He told me he had reported all my comments! On the whole I had an enjoyable tenure in the US and got on with most of my colleagues. I was most impressed by the vitality of the American people for whom I developed great respect.

I had brought with me the mounted head and skin of a leopard that I had earlier shot. The trophy was mounted in Mysore by Van Ingen and Van Ingen. Unfortunately one of the teeth had broken in transit. I took it down to a dentist in Lawton. Initially he feigned to be insulted at being asked to fix a leopard's tooth, but after a brief discussion he agreed to fix it at a price. I presented the trophy to the commandant, and it was mounted and displayed in Snow Hall. Incidentally, the lady liaison officer for foreign officers asked me to give the trophy to her, and did not conceal her displeasure when I declined.

I had perforce to study hard on the course as weekly mark-sheets were displayed for all to see. My final percentage results were well into the nineties. There was much explaining to do on my return to India on one of the remarks on my course report: 'An aggressive officer.' This was meant to be a compliment but the military hierarchy in India took 'aggressive' to mean 'quarrelsome'. I had found that the Indian military hierarchy was more interested in compliant malleability rather than an aggressive outlook. Unfortunately, this attitude continues to obtain in the armed forces today: initiative on the part of junior officers is not appreciated by their seniors.

During my stay in the US, I attended a talk by Glubb Pasha who I had met earlier in Iraq. The lecture glorified his Arab legion and their role in the Second World War, and later against the Haganah in Palestine. I reminded him of our earlier meeting in Iraq and told him I did not approve of his anti-Semitic views. Glubb, like many other British Arabist officers, was a committed anti-Israeli Arabist.

After the course I drove down to Fort Bragg for a liaison visit. Brig. Gen. Stillwell, son of 'Vinegar' Joe Stillwell was in command. We had long discussions. I had met 'Vinegar' Joe in India at Ramgarh where there was a training establishment for the Chinese troops of Chiang Kai-shek's army. Sadly, Brig. Gen. Stillwell died later in an air mishap en route to Pearl Harbour. Lord Louis Mountbatten was visiting Fort Bragg at that time. At a banquet hosted in his honour, Mountbatten wore the uniform of an admiral of the fleet. He noticed me in my Indian army blue patrols and signalled me to sit beside him. He spoke of his love for India and his role as governor general and, later, viceroy. He discussed the Ramree operation in which I had participated and recounted that the original task given to 26 Indian Division was to retake the Andaman Islands. The Intelligence was given the task of simulating an attack on Ramree in the area of Mount Peter. The plan was later changed and the objective became the island of Ramree. The Intelligence was not informed of the change and continued to simulate a landing on Ramree Island. Fortunately the landing took place at Kyakpau and not Mount Peter. He also recalled the incident of the booing of Maj. Gen. Chambers, and his visit to

Ramree to boost morale. He was amused when I told him that the soldiers of my regiment called him 'Lord Mountain Battery'.

I sold my car at Fort Bragg for $200 and spent a few enjoyable days in New York. I stayed in a hotel off Central Park, which charged $12 a day for the room. Returning to London on the *Queen Mary*, we embarked to return to India on an Anchor Lines vessel. In August 1960 I arrived back in India and was told to report to the Artillery School as chief instructor, tactics. I had barely settled down when orders came to report to HQ, Western Command to take up the key assignment of general staff officer, operations grade 1 or GSO1 (Ops) as it is generally called.

The army commander was Lt Gen. P.N. Thapar, an upright and cultured man, and the brigadier, General Staff, was Brig. Dewan Prem Chand, a competent and personable officer. We got on extremely well. I took many decisions without reference to the army commander and was marched up several times. Prem stood by me. Major differences arose between the army commander and me regarding the defence of Ladakh, with particular reference to the so called 'forward policy'. I stressed that any forward deployment was contingent on building up the infrastructure and logistics. Krishna Menon and other politicians were pressing for a forward deployment policy. The matter was left unresolved. The army commander proposed some radical changes to the organization of artillery units. I wrote on the file that we should not consider such 'bastard' organizations. I was summoned. General Thapar then ordered me to delete what he described as abusive language. I declined and retorted that if he did not like my note he could reject it. It stayed on the file. Fortunately for me, in April 1961 I was asked for by Maj. Gen. Sam Manekshaw to go to the Staff College as an instructor. I had known Manekshaw earlier when he was director of military operations at Army Headquarters, and was a frequent visitor to his bungalow in King George's Avenue (now known as Rajaji Marg). Lt Col Jangoo Sataravala, who was awarded the Military Cross for gallantry in the Italian campaign, often came there. Sam Manekshaw initially liked Sataravala, but many years later fell out with him.

I reported to Manekshaw, and he briefed me on my duties and told me to take up residence at Wellington Club. The club is situated in a valley and had a nine-hole hill golf course. The old squash court had been converted into two residential quarters. I had the top floor, the secretary the bottom. The work-load on an instructor at the Staff College is heavy. Not only has he to study and prepare his lessons but also to correct numerous papers and exercises. There were excellent facilities for games and sports. Riding with the Ootacamund Hunt on the downs was enjoyable, as were the amateur horse races. I managed to get my golf handicap down to twelve. Manekshaw played no games nor rode to hounds. His only outdoor recreation was fishing.

I had to revise several of the exercises set for the course students. One particularly outdated one was on mountain warfare, which was probably the same one that had been used by the college in Quetta before it moved to Wellington, and was based on the techniques of picketing used in the North - West frontier during the 1920s and '30s. I rewrote and reset the exercise and chose the locale of Bombdi La, a place which was to figure prominently during the Chinese invasion of 1962. Manekshaw, unlike Lentaigne, did not take an active part in the tactical discussions. He did however introduce the lectures of VIPs. Being a bachelor, I was asked to dine with these VIPs in order to make up an even number at the table. Mrs Silloo Manekshaw was a charming lady, considerate and gracious. She kept a very good table, was kind to me, and I will always cherish her memory.

Manekshaw got into deep trouble at the college. He had the habit of speaking out of turn and making disparaging remarks about the heroes of Indian history. He did little to conceal his fondness for all things Western, and his antipathy towards the government's foreign and domestic policies. Reports of these criticisms began reaching Delhi and cognizance was taken of his indiscreet outbursts. A court of enquiry was ordered by the defence minister, Krishna Menon. Manekshaw was accused of being anti-national. The principal movers in the campaign against him were Krishna Menon and his protégé Lt Gen. Kaul. Kaul considered Manekshaw to be a potential rival and was busy gathering evidence against him to support the charges. One evening when I was having dinner at the residence of one of my colleagues, Lt Col Fateh Shinde, I received a phone call from a staff officer to Kaul asking me to give evidence against Manekshaw. The evidence they wanted was Manekshaw's intemperate remarks to me and Lt Col Zoru Bakshi. Bakshi had just left for an assignment to the Congo and was not available. I was informed that if I gave this evidence, I could have any assignment I desired and that my future career would be secure. The remarks in question were indiscreet, derogatory, and could be used to support the charges being levied. I declined. Kaul then came on the line and asked me to reconsider, telling me that if I did not comply my career would be in jeopardy! I politely refused as I found reporting on my boss unethical, and at the same time had little respect for Kaul. I was to later discover that Kaul had my position at the top of the seniority list moved down to the bottom!

Later, I earned the ire of Manekshaw over a British planter's complaint that I had had the audacity to evict him, an important member of the British community, from the club. Manekshaw demanded an explanation. I told him that the planter was drunk, abusive, and making a nuisance of himself. This did not satisfy him. I told him that I had earlier indicated to him that I did not wish to take on the assignment of honorary secretary, and that too in my spare time, and that if this planter misbehaved again I would have no hesitation in evicting him. I added that as he was unhappy with my conduct as honorary secretary I was resigning with immediate effect. Manekshaw was livid. He told me that I would have to continue until further orders. Fortunately for me a paid secretary was appointed shortly afterwards.

Manekshaw's habit of making loose comments was to continue. An astonishing document released by the US State Department (*see* Appendix) mentions his conversation with William K. Hitchcock, American Consul General, Calcutta, on 12 October 1966 on a flight from Calcutta to Delhi. Manekshaw was then Eastern Army Commander. He revealed his frank discussions with the defence minister, his views on Indo-Pak relations, Kashmir, Bhutan, the Chogyal of Sikkim, and his anti-Soviet and pro-Western orientation. He said that he could not openly admit to being pro-Western because that would thwart his prospects of becoming army chief and consequently to redirect military thinking away from the Soviets. He criticized the army chief, Gen. Chaudhuri's, conduct of the 1965 war with Pakistan. Hitchcock was surprised when Manekshaw told him that the Indians allowed the Chinese through a few menancing rounds to pin down the 300,000 troops he had under his command, thus confirming to the Americans the strength of our Eastern Army. This report was circulated to all American embassies in the region. Manekshaw had been in combat for a brief spell in Burma during the withdrawal across the Sittang bridge, was wounded and awarded the Military Cross which he rightly deserved. Other than in 1942, Manekshaw saw no other combat. Manekshaw's flair for the dramatic is best reflected in the oft-told story that Maj. Gen. 'Punch' Cowan, the divisional commander, saw him lying wounded, and pinned his own Military Cross on him, saying that a dead person cannot be awarded such a medal! (*Tribune,* 13 January 2005). Medals were not worn in operations in a combat zone and therefore Gen. Cowan could not have been wearing any.

Manekshaw also regaled audiences with stories of his 'exchanges' with Mrs Indira Gandhi many years after she was assassinated. It was widely known that he used to defer to each and every wish of hers. He repeated stories about his exchanges with Mrs Gandhi, loving to build on his charismatic persona, a creation largely of a doting press. In 1997, I published my account of the 1971 war in my book *Surrender at Dacca: Birth of a Nation.* I gave copies to Manekshaw and J.S. Aurora in 1997 when they were both in good health and active. Neither of them countered or contradicted what I had written in the book. Manekshaw's only comment then to me was: 'Why did you put that horrible picture of me in the book?'

In all fairness, Mankeshaw established a good rapport with the bureaucracy and stood up to them when necessary. He did more than any other chief to maintain the dignity of the army. Despite our many differences, I have the highest regard for Manekshaw. He was kind and considerate to me as was his charming wife. Unfortunately, after the publication of my book *Surrender at Dacca* in 1997, our relationship became strained. Manekshaw had merely glanced through the book that I had given him. Extracts, out of context, were shown to him. These, he felt were incompatible with the aura his public relations media campaign had created that he, single-handed, controlled all operations from his office in South Block. After the war, while still in service, he gave an interview to a British newspaper asserting that if he had been the Pakistani army chief in 1971, Pakistan would have won the war! Mrs Gandhi was furious and despite consistent lobbying by Manekshaw and others to appoint him field marshal, agreed most reluctantly a few weeks before his retirement on a pension with no perks!

Gen. Thimayya on retirement had perforce to take on the role of secretary of the United Planters' Association of Southern India in Coonoor, as the government declined to give him a suitable appointment. Thimayya often dropped in for a drink at my quarters at the Club and I was often invited to his bungalow. He behaved with great dignity but was bitter about the shabby treatment meted out to him by the politicians. He discussed with me the operations of his brigade in Burma, as also his pivotal role in operations in Jammu & Kashmir, particularly the classic one at Zoji La. Later, Thimayya's capabilities were eventually recognized and he was given a prestigious command in the United Nations Peace Keeping Operations. He was indeed a 'man for all seasons'.

After the 1962 Chinese invasion, Manekshaw was promoted to the rank of Lt. General and appointed the corps commander of 4 Corps in Eastern Command. At a farewell party at the Wellington Gymkhana Club, I recall Silloo Manekshaw telling Sam to thank me for not giving evidence against him. Manekshaw did not respond and moved away. Manekshaw was extremely fortunate to escape so lightly from the anti-national charges filed against him.

From the Staff College I was posted as Colonel Q, Southern Command in Poona (or Pune as it is now called). Others who were earlier lower down in the promotion list were promoted to the rank of brigadier and went on to command brigades! This was obviously related to the Kaul incident! I handed my resignation papers to the army commander who refused to accept them, saying he would come back to me. Later he told me that he had spoken to the military secretary who told him that my promotion had been delayed due to my earlier request to be sent to an operational area, and as one would fall vacant soon I would be promoted soon. Regretfully I believed him then, but was much later to discover that this was a blatant lie, but by then it was too late.

6

Stints in Ladakh and Deolali

The Southern Army Commander (GOC-in-C, Southern Command, Lt Gen. L.P. ('Bogey') Sen, whom I had earlier known in Burma, was a pucca brown sahib. He was more interested in attending the races in Bombay and Pune than in attending office or visiting combat units and formations. One of my more difficult assignments was to find him establishments to visit in Bombay so that he could attend the race meetings during the racing season. Sen took little interest in matters of administration, delegating his powers to me. This gave me an opportunity to plan and initiate works to house the units of the southern army. I was able to build the Artillery Centre in Golconda near Hyderabad and make up for deficiencies in accommodation at the Artillery Centre in Nasik. I made a mistake in sanctioning parade grounds in both centres of a size of 400 x 400 yards. I had to do a lot of explaining about the parameters I had used to sanction such large parade grounds. These parade grounds, possibly the largest in any country, are today fully utilized. We built accommodation in various locations in order to cater to the expansion of the army in the aftermath of the 1962 war.

I was given promotion to the rank of brigadier and assigned to assume command of 3 Artillery Brigade in Ladakh. Ladakh in 1963 was considered to be a difficult assignment. There was hardly any infrastructure and troops had to construct their own accommodation. In addition to my brigade, I was also station commander at Leh. Ladakh is a high altitude desert, with mountain ranges that are stark and steep. Other than some scrub in the river-beds there is little vegetation. The major river, the Indus, flows from Tibet through a broad valley. There are many lakes, the largest being the Pangong which lies partly on our side of the line of control and partly in the Chinese occupied area. The water on our side is brackish whereas it is sweet on the Chinese side. The area is rich in wildlife: ibex, wild sheep, wild asses, antelope, a few snow leopards, and also a variety of birds (chukor, pheasant and duck). There are a large number of monasteries, the most important being the Red Hat monastery of Hemis belonging to the Red Hat sect of Tibetan Buddhism. Hemis is tucked into a small valley and is not visible from the main route along the Indus River. This was indeed fortunate because Gulab Singh, in his invasion of Tibet, is alleged to have looted several monasteries en route; Hemis was fortunately spared in consequence.

Kushok Bakulla headed the Yellow Sect of Tibetan Buddhism in Ladakh and his monastery was located at Spituk. We became good friends. The divisional commander of the infantry division in Ladakh when I arrived was suffering from gout and did not move out of his headquarters. This gave me the freedom to visit all areas on his behalf, from the Karakoram pass in the west to where the Indus enters in the east.

I stayed some two years in Ladakh, in what proved to be one of my most enjoyable assignments. The summers were idyllic, the winters severe. I spent a considerable time out of Leh, visiting units as also the numerous monasteries. I came to respect the Buddhist culture and was impressed by the dedication of the monks.

I was asked to prepare a detailed assessment of the potential Chinese threat and the counter-measures that needed to be taken. In my view, the Chinese will never vacate the Aksai Chin as their road communications to Sinkiang (Xinjiang) Pass through it. In retrospect, I recall my brief tenure as GSO1, Operations, Western Command, and my recommendations regarding building up the infrastructure, particularly the roads, before moving the troops forward. We took a beating in Ladakh as well as in Arunachal in 1962. Fortunately, some lessons have been learnt. A build up of the infrastructure and logistics are essential elements for both offensive and defensive operations. It was the experience of the 1962 debacle that I had in mind when I resisted Manekshaw's persistent badgering to move into Bangladesh in April 1971 without preparing the infrastructure and logistics to sustain operations.

There was a Moravian Christian Mission building surrounded by Lombardy poplars on the outskirts of Leh in which was housed the office of the Divisional Headquarters. I initiated a project to plant poplar and willow at all army locations all over Ladakh, and took cuttings and distributed them to units to plant. Today, Ladakh is a much greener place.

After two years I was assigned to assume command of the artillery school in Deolali. I arrived in Deolali early in 1965; it had not changed much since my earlier assignments. There were the same old classrooms in huts, and the gun-sheds around the gun park were on the verge of collapse. Funding for construction was very restricted; but we nonetheless managed to get a new officers' mess as well as bachelor and married accommodation constructed. These works had been sanctioned earlier by me in 1963 when I was posted in Poona. I presented a large part of my art and weapons collection to the officers' mess where they are now displayed.

Deolali is my favourite cantonment in India. I was commissioned into the artillery there, served as an instructor, gunnery, and later for a brief spell as chief instructor, tactics, and eventually became commandant. I loved the rolling green plateau dominated by steep, stark hills with names such as Bahula, with a Maratha fort on its crest, Pandulena, famous for its temple, and Siva Donga on the outskirts of the cantonment.

War clouds were looming on the horizon in 1965. We were on the verge of war with Pakistan. Soon hostilities broke out. We had an infantry brigade in Barmer in Rajasthan which was taking a pounding. The southern army commander at Poona, Gen. Gopal Beewor, phoned me requesting that I send him some guns to help the brigade (commanded by Brig. Summanwar). I explained that I came under Army HQ, who I knew would not agree to such a request. He again explained the urgency of the situation. I agreed to send a mixed ad hoc regiment of field and medium guns manned by personnel of the artillery school. I moved with this ad hoc regiment to Barmer but had to return to Deolali disappointed that I could not stay with this regiment and fight. The war ended inconclusively. A great deal of unpleasantness with the director of artillery, Maj. Gen. Naravane was to follow. In any event, we were not on the best of terms. He was furious with me for earlier declining to accept the 75 mm pack howitzer; he was steering its development and hoped to get it into service. During the acceptance trials there were 98 defects, some very major: the muzzle brake flew off and the sight bracket snapped. He told me to agree to pass it and said that he would subsequently correct the defects. I explained that I could only pass the gun after it had physically passed its trials. There were other trials with smoke ammunition that we were not able to clear. He gave me a very poor annual confidential report, and despite this I was later promoted.

General Kumaramangalam visited the school. He told me that I would have to stay on as he could not find a replacement for me. This meant that I would not be able to get a tenure as a commander of an infantry brigade, a prerequisite for commanding a division. I told Gen. Kumaramangalam that it was fine by me because the regiment came first. After the completion of his visit to Deolali, Gen. Kumaramangalam after ascending the steps of his aircraft, descended and called me aside. He told me he had reconsidered and that he would send me to command an infantry brigade. I moved shortly after to command 168 Infantry Brigade in Samba, near Jammu. The post of commandant of the school had remained vacant for over three months and the officer posted to command it in my place did not have the necessary qualifications in gunnery to command it. I will always cherish the memory of Gen. Kumaramangalam to whom I do indeed owe a great deal.

My tenure in Samba was to be tempestuous. There were many unresolved problems on the alignment of the border stretching from Pathankot to Jammu. I was fortunate that my opposite number on the Pakistani side was Brig. Azmat Hayat, the son of Sir Sikander Hayat, and together we demarcated the border. Pakistan would not agree to placing concrete pillars so, and as a compromise, we half embedded earth-filled forty gallon gasoline drums. I attended the border meetings with no paraphernalia. Brig. Hayat, on the other hand, had only to clap his hands and the locals would set up a shamiana with carpets and sofas. The internal prestige and power of the Pakistan military was enormous. Unfortunately, the general commanding our division (26 Infantry Division), and I had different perspectives. He loved his liquor and insisted that my officers and their wives should attend the numerous parties in the officers' club in Jammu. The brigade officers and their wives were not keen to drive for almost two hours on a bumpy road and preferred to attend our local club. This displeased the divisional commander.

The 16th Battalion, Central Reserve Police (CRP) a central para-military force, was responsible for patrolling the border. In their patrolling they had taken a short cut, cutting off a sizeable chunk of Pakistani territory. When the Pakistanis discovered this, there was considerable agitation and heated exchanges between the Pakistani Rangers and the CRP. In anticipation of problems, I moved two companies of 1/1 Gorkha Rifles, one of my three infantry battalions, to a location nearby. The divisional commander wanted to see the area; so I took him to a position nearby and pointed it out. We had only a small escort of the CRP, one junior commissioned officer and one constable. The general said that he wanted to walk the length of the area in dispute. I told him that this was not advisable as I had not brought a proper escort. The two companies of Gorkhas were over a mile away. He retorted that his counterpart in Pakistan and he were on very good terms and no Pakistani would dare interfere with him. I told him that the Pakistani Rangers were in an aggressive mood, in response to which he made a taunting remark. We then proceeded along the disputed patrol beat. After a few hundred yards we were confronted by a group of Rangers. They told us to go back. These Rangers fortunately knew me and after explaining the purpose of our visit to them they allowed us to proceed. A few hundred yards ahead we were confronted by another group of Rangers. They demanded we go back. The general then shouted out not to take any notice as they would do nothing to him. Immediately they raised their rifles. The general then bolted into the tall grass. I faced the Rangers and tried to reason with them. At a range of 25 yards they fired, grazing the turban of the inspector on my left, and hitting Constable Harphool, who was on my right, in the stomach. I was fortunate that they hit my walking stick. I took a roll into the long grass, dragging constable Harphool with me. The inspector lay feigning to be dead. I picked up the constable's rifle and bandolier and began firing at the Rangers who then withdrew. I told the constable to lie there and that I would come back for him.

I crawled through the grass to where the general was taking refuge. Meanwhile, a Pakistani machine gun located in a concrete bunker some 500 yard inside Pakistan began firing at us. I began to return the fire but was stopped by the general who told me not to draw fire. I told the general that I would make a dash to where the two companies of Gorkhas were located and that he should follow. He retorted that he was an infantry officer and would use field-craft to return, that is, crawl. I snapped back that I was a gunner and would make a dash. I reached the Gorkha companies and we went in the cleared area and brought back the two wounded personnel of the CRP. Late in the evening, the general phoned me for a report. I briefed him about the subsequent events. He then said that as the machine gun in the Pakistani bunker on the other side of the international border had dared to open fire on him, I must attack the bunker and destroy it. I pointed out that the bunker was well within Pakistani territory and that the approach to it was over open ground. Firstly, if we attacked it it would be an act of war, secondly, it would result in heavy casualties for my troops. He angrily responded that he did not care how many causalities we would sustain but that the bunker should be destroyed and he went on to imply that I was getting cold feet! This enraged me. I said that such an order was totally illegal and I would not comply. Further, if he did not care how many casualties we sustained I, on the contrary, would under no circumstances sacrifice the lives of my jawans for such an infructuous and futile operation. He rudely suggested that I was scared. I replied that it was he who by his lack of judgment had precipitated the firing incident, and that on being confronted by the Pakistani Rangers lost his nerve and bolted leaving me and two CRP personnel to face the Pakistani Rangers. He then made other sarcastic remarks. I could take it no longer. I told him that his behaviour was cowardly and that if he wished I would confirm what I had said in writing, that his actions were those of a coward. I made some other derogatory remarks regarding his cowardice. I was at that juncture quite prepared to resign my commission on the issue.

Two days later, I received a call to meet the GOC. I met him in his office. He began giving me a lecture on his parameters of command. I responded that I was not interested in his parameters and I was prepared to give him in writing that I had described his behaviour as that of a coward; also the circumstances of his precipitating the incident and then bolting. He then said that he had thought I was one of them, reminding me too that my annual confidential report was due. I reiterated that I would not retract my statement and that he could do whatever he thought fit. That brought the meeting to a close. Incidentally, he later gave me an excellent annual confidential report! Presumably he developed cold feet.

For the record, I had written a long report to the Division on the incident which they did not forward. Later, the brigade major, Maj. Baraich, before leaving his assignment, requested me to destroy the office copy; I told him he could do so. Many years later in 1974, when I was the eastern army commander based at HQ Eastern Command, Kolkata, and visiting Nagaland, the 16 CRP battalion was presenting me with a guard of honour. Suddenly one of the policemen broke ranks, rushed forward, and hugged me. It was Harphool!

A few days later the GOC passed by my office in Samba on his way out to avail casual leave. He told me that a communal riot was brewing in Jammu and as he was proceeding on casual leave, I, as the senior brigade commander, was to take over command and sort out the problem. He then left.

I proceeded to Jammu and met the commissioner and the deputy commissioner (DC). The commissioner had handed over the situation to the army as he had been hit by a brick. The DC, Thakkar, told the commissioner that he, the commissioner, was not empowered to hand over the situation to the army as the authority for this lay with the DC and not the commissioner. The commissioner then left. I told the DC that I had ordered two companies of infantry to a location nearby, as a precautionary measure. I recalled a somewhat similar incident in Leh in 1964 when a Ladakhi mob was bent on attacking another community. I reasoned with them and they dispersed.

The DC and I went to approach the mob. They were in an aggressive mood. The mob was armed with spears, swords, and bricks and were bent on attacking the minority community. I went forward to address them. The atmosphere was tense and some more bricks were hurled; I reasoned with the mob but they continued shouting slogans. After some fifteen minutes they quietened down and slowly dispersed. I then handed back the situation to the DC and not the commissioner. The DC displayed courage and 'guts' throughout. It was indeed fortunate that the mob dispersed peacefully.

During my tenure as brigade commander I practised moving the brigade group using subsidiary dirt tracks as well as cross country. It was a learning curve for me as well as for the brigade. I had always stressed mobility and manoeuvre. The Indian army's normal manoeuvre pattern was to move along a road axis with its logistic support following, and it was essential that we broke away from this rigid practice. Later, on my next assignment as a major general commanding 12 Infantry Division in Rajasthan, we further developed the techniques of moving on subsidiary tracks as well as cross country, only later opening up the logistical axes of maintenance. We developed the techniques of bypassing centres of resistance, selecting communication and command centres as objectives rather than towns. This strategy we put in place during the operations in 1971. In 1969, as general officer commanding, 12 Infantry Division, I prepared a training manual on desert warfare which was incorporated in the army manual on desert warfare.

The 12 Infantry Division was in the process of being raised in the area of Jodhpur and neighbouring cantonments in Rajasthan. The general assigned to command it fell ill shortly after assuming command, so I was left to complete the raising.

I enjoyed my tenure in Rajasthan. We came directly under HQ, Southern Command. The army commander was Lt Gen. Moti Sagar, who had been my instructor as platoon commander of the cadet platoon when I was an officer cadet at Mhow. He was an upright, competent officer and a thorough gentleman, and gave me a free hand to train the division.

We had no navigation devices, and this hindered our cross country movement. I developed a method of navigation from a moving vehicle using a magnetic compass mounted on a gimbal. The magnetic variation varied with the direction. We then prepared a variation graph for 360° of the compass for the navigating vehicle. This device was in use by both 11 and 12 Infantry Divisions until it was replaced by modern navigation devices.

We trained to operate cross country, emphasis being on shock action and mobility. I learnt a great deal from the numerous training manoeuvres we held, and this was to stand me in good stead later in planning for operations in 1971.

My tenure in Jodphur was most enjoyable. I got to love the desert, particularly the area around Jaisalmer. My aide-de-camp Capt. Riar and I drove around the complete area and prepared a 'going map' indicating the motorability of the terrain for wheeled and tracked vehicles. I prepared outline plans for defensive and offensive operations and realized the importance of Longewala and the Ramgarh axis. Before I left I had 4000 anti-tank mines dumped at Longewala anticipating that this was a likely thrust line for the Pakistan army. These mines were not laid prior to the 1971 operations. Fortunately for us the Pakistani armoured thrust got bogged down near Longewala presenting lucrative targets for our air force.

The house for the division commander, Senapati House, formerly the residence of the commander of the Jodhpur State Forces before their integration into the Indian Army, was spacious. It had a swimming pool and two tennis courts. There were no facilities for an army club in Jodhpur, so I converted the area of the swimming pool and tennis courts into a club for the officers of the division and the officers of the air force station.

Shortly after assuming command I received a phone call from B.N. Elias of the B.N. Elias Group of Industries, National Tobacco, Agarpara Jute, etc to meet with them in Calcutta. One of my close relatives was a partner in the company. B.N. Elias, the last of the proprietors, wanted to leave India and asked me to resign from the army and take over the group on their behalf. I told them that I would complete my service, and only then would I be prepared to take over the group but they wanted me to resign immediately. I declined and I am glad I did. Many years earlier, at the end of the Second World War, one of the officers of my regiment, David Mudie, son of Sir Francis

Mudie, former governor of Punjab, offered me the most attractive terms to join Burma Shell. I had declined then too. David Mudie was to rise to the top of Burma Shell worldwide. You do not get rich in the army, but for me an army career is beyond compare.

In May 1969, I received a phone call from Manekshaw saying he was soon to become the chief of the army staff and would be relinquishing the appointment of army commander, Eastern Command. He said that he was going to have me posted as chief of staff, eastern command. He added that he knew that I would not like to work as his staff officer as earlier I had requested him not to have me posted as his brigadier general, staff. He said that I would have to tolerate him for a fortnight and I replied that a fortnight was acceptable. He then said that Jagjit Singh Aurora was to be the army commander, eastern command and that he had very little confidence in him. I asked him why, if that was the case, was he sending him there. He replied: 'I like to have him as a doormat'.

I have a special bond with Calcutta, the city where I was born. The people of Calcutta are cultured, warm, and friendly. I moved into Watergate House in Fort William. It was a large sprawling house built in 1780 on the ramparts of the fort and had a magnificent view of the River Hooghli. The water from the river flooded through the water-gate into the moat, the house being astride the gate. I had known the fort from my boyhood. Two of the army boys from my school, Brogan and Burnett, often called me over and took me around. Nothing much in the fort seemed to have changed, except that the British battalion and headquarters had been replaced by Indian ones.

I began taking over as chief of staff from Maj. Gen. Shankaran Nair, who was one of Manekshaw's coterie. Manekshaw, in one of our conversations, had complained about the West Bengal government demanding a very large sum of money to transfer Field Marshal Lord Roberts' statue to the regimental centre of the Fifth Gurkhas. I responded that Roberts was a gunner, a master gunner, and if the statue had to go to any regiment it should go to the artillery. He replied that Roberts had been a honorary colonel of the Fifth Gurkhas. I was quite taken aback by his next remark. 'You know, I have another reason. Roberts was known as "Bobs Bahadur" throughout the British Army, and I am known as Sam Bahadur by all the Gurkhas and the whole of the Indian Army'. I responded that I had not heard anyone call him 'Sam Bahadur'. The British soldiers were more informal, the Indian soldier would not take such liberties, and would address him as Manekshaw Sahib or *Huzoor*. He then called Maj. Gen. Nair and asked directly, 'Shankaran, doesn't the whole Indian Army call me Sam Bahadur?' to which Shankaran replied, 'Yes sir; yes sir the whole Indian Army calls you Sam Bahadur'. Roberts was commissioned in the Bengal artillery and was awarded the Victoria Cross. He personally led several cavalry charges in Afghanistan. He was loved and respected by all the rank and file. After being wounded in Burma, Manekshaw served on the staff and never physically commanded a Gorkha battalion or any battalion of the army. The Sam Bahadur nickname was subsequently perpetuated by Manekshaw and lapped up by the media.

With the change of government in Writer's Building, I requested the state government, who were removing British statues, to donate Roberts' equestrian statue to the Regiment of Artillery. They did not ask for any money for the statue, only removal charges. Field Marshal Roberts of Kandahar, VC, Bengal Artillery and master gunner seated astride his charger at the entrance of the Artillery Centre at Nasik Road, rides proudly to this day.

Manekshaw left to take over as chief of army staff, taking Shankaran Nair as the director of staff duties at Army Headquarters. I soon settled down. Aurora was fairly easy to get on with. Working hours at Command HQ were officially 7.30 a.m. to 1.30 p.m. Aurora generally arrived at 10 o'clock. Around 12 o'clock his wife Bhanti Aurora arrived at his office. They had tea and left shortly after for luncheon engagements hosted by the various business houses. Aurora soon became part of the social circuit. This paved the way for his employment by a prominent Calcutta business house on his retirement.

There were law and order problems in West Bengal. The Naxalite movement, which began in Naxalbari in North Bengal, was gaining momentum. Elections were due to be held. A communist 'United Front' government was in power. We were visited by the army chief Gen. Manekshaw and the Union Home Secretary Govind Narain. The army commander, J.S. Aurora, was away at Darjeeling. Manekshaw told me that the government was very concerned about the worsening law and order situation, particularly in view of the upcoming elections. He then directed that eastern command should smash the Naxalite movement and that we would be responsible for providing security for the elections. I replied, as any officer would have, that it was not our responsibility but that of the state government and police. Govind Narain then responded that the situation was not under control and that if we did not do so, it would get completely out of control. Manekshaw then chipped in, 'You will bloody well do it. You will be directly responsible to me for carrying out this task.' I said that if so ordered I would do so. I paused for a minute or so, reviewing the problems of implementing this order, and then told them that we had adequate troops in north Bengal, but I would require two divisions for the rest of Bengal. Sam was generous, and said, 'Done, I will give you the two divisions and I am also going to give you 50 Para Brigade as well. I expect results. You will, in case of any difficultly, phone me.' I asked him to send this in writing. To this he retorted brusquely that there was no need for written orders and that his verbal instructions were based on the orders of Prime Minister Indira Gandhi who had nominated me to command the operation.

He then put his arm around me and said, 'Jake, I have full confidence in you, I want results. You can inform Aurora.' Manekshaw true to his word sent us 9 Infantry and 4 Mountain Divisions as also 50 Parachute Brigade. Together with GOC 33 Corps, whose HQ was located in north Bengal and HQ Bengal Area which was located in Calcutta, we worked out deployment and operational plans. Elections were held and the army was deployed right down to polling booths. A Congress government took over. Chief Minister Siddharth Shankar Ray and Commissioner of Police Calcutta, Ranjit Gupta, provided intelligence and police resources. The combined efforts of all ensured that, by the end of 1971, the back of the Naxalite movement in West Bengal was all but broken. The movement has re-emerged in other states and unfortunately the various state governments are unable to cope, and there is little coordination between them. Unless the counter-insurgency operations are handed over to the army the movement will spread further. Credit for ordering operations in West Bengal should also go to Prime Minister Indira Gandhi, the defence minister, the home minister, and Manekshaw who provided the troops, Siddhartha

Shankar Ray and Ranjit Gupta of the police ,and the soldiers who participated. Incidentally, Manekshaw, after giving me verbal orders took no further interest in these operations. Siddhartha Shankar Ray told all and sundry: 'Jake and I, we broke the Naxals.'

Unfortunately, Charu Mazumdar, who began the movement, died in prison. He was coming around to arriving at a solution. The Naxalites displayed great courage. I recall one incident when one of our patrols was moving near Barrackpore. A Naxalite armed with a one shot pipegun shot dead the patrol commander and was immediately gunned down.

On another occasion, on one of my visits to troops engaged in anti-naxal operations, my driver lost his way near Behala. A group of Naxalites, armed with knives and spears, surrounded the car. Fortunately, I was carrying my .38 Smith and Wesson revolver and I fired over their heads, dispersing them. They then allowed us to proceed on our way.

Insurgencies in Nagaland and Mizoram were growing in intensity. I was too involved with the counter-Naxalite operations to spare much time for these areas, and we were soon to become involved with the events in Bangladesh.

In September 1970 I had accompanied Manekshaw on a goodwill visit to the Soviet Union as guests of Soviet Defence Minister Marshal Grechko. Manekshaw checked with the Soviet Ambassador whether I, as a Jew, would be acceptable. He got a sharp reply from the Soviets that Jacob was more than welcome and that there were numerous Jewish generals in their army, many of them decorated as heroes of the Soviet Union. Manekshaw also took his wife and ADC along with him. We had a most instructive and enjoyable visit. As state guests we were comfortably housed, dined, and lavishly entertained and had a special aircraft at our disposal. I got first hand exposure to how the 'rich' lived. The Soviets refused to provide us with batmen on the plea that communists do not use soldiers as batmen. Inadvertently I entered the room where Lt Gen. Kupriano, our liaison officer, was staying and saw two soldiers attending to him, one taking off his boots. I said, 'Kupriano no batmen,' and he turned red. Manekshaw's ADC doubled up as his batman. I had no need for one and did my own chores. We were ushered into the presence of Marshal Grechko. On a side table there was a long strip map of the Suez Canal with the positions of Egyptian and Israeli troops marked. Our talks were frequently interrupted by phone calls updating the minister on events there. He talked at length on China and the dangers they posed not only for India but also for the Soviet Union. He dwelt on the border problems they had with China. He said that the Soviets had sent a satellite up to check on the progress of construction of the Chinese road through Aksai Chin. We were taken aback by his concluding remark, 'You cannot trust the Chinese; they are not gentlemen!'.

We visited the famous Tamanski division on the outskirts of Moscow. They had arranged a demonstration of the division in assault, with live firing which was most impressive. They showed us around their barracks. The conscripts, though ill paid, were then well fed. This was the division that put Boris Yeltsin back in power.

We went round some other installations where we were shown tanks, armoured personnel carriers, and other items of equipment. Manekshaw had earlier discussed with me that he wanted to buy some old upgraded Centurion tanks. I strongly protested that it made little sense to buy old obsolete tanks from South Africa when we could get new modern tanks from Russia. I told him that the T-55 on offer was robust and 'idiot' proof. It was, besides, descended from the T-34, the most efficient tank produced during the Second World War. I also suggested he should go in for the armoured personnel carriers and the Grad family of missiles. He said he would consider my suggestions, and did take my advice and we opted for the T-55, armoured personnel carriers, and the Grad P missile. The armoured personnel carriers arrived just prior to the 1971 war as did the Grad P missile.

From Moscow we went to the city of Leningrad, now once again St Petersburg. Leningrad is a beautiful city; I loved the Hermitage museum. There we met Marshal Zakharoff who, as a private soldier, took part in the assault on the summer palace during the Russian Revolution. He regaled us with stories of his experiences and proved a very likeable individual. I was most impressed by the war memorials both at Leningrad and Moscow. The Russians really honour those who have given their lives for their country, and we in India should follow their example and do much more. One of Zakharoff's remarks to me regarding the use of helicopters was that they were meant for logistical rather than offensive operations as was the case with the Americans in Vietnam. History has proved him wrong.

In my conversations with the Russian generals, I found they were not conversant with their pre-Soviet history. In Borodino Museum I mentioned to our escorting general that Katuzoff was also in command of the Allied Forces at Austerlitz during the war against Napoleon. They seemed wholly unaware of this. Later, they feigned ignorance of the role of Prince Menshikoff in the Crimean war.

We also visited Kiev, and a collective farm nearby which failed to impress me in the slightest and appeared quite unproductive. I suggested that they get some of our farmers from the Punjab to help to improve production, a suggestion to which they did not take at all kindly. Wherever we went I was impressed by the way they looked after their historic monuments. We were taken to their holiday resort in the Crimea. Throughout, our movements were closely monitored. For instance, in Moscow I had arranged with some friends who lived there to see the city with them. The plan was that after a ballet at the Kremlin, I would break away and meet them outside the Kremlin gate. I thought I had got away with it, but as I neared the gate I felt a hand on my shoulder and a voice asked: 'Where are you going?' I was escorted back to the group much to Manekshaw's amusement.

The entertainment and banquets were fabulous. There were four meals a day with mounds of Beluga Caviar. Russian wines are sweet, but the vodka dry. During my numerous toasts at the banquets, I managed to swap my Vodka glasses with one's for water, as the general beside me, a Jew and a twice-decorated hero of the Soviet Union, was also doing. I noticed that they invariably sent Jewish generals to meet and escort me.

Manekshaw kept downing vodka and was often under its influence. At one such banquet, standing unsteadily, he repeated the same speech at the initial and subsequent toasts, much to the amusement of the Russians.

In the Crimea, early one morning, I evaded my minders and went down to the beach. The Russians are an extremely friendly and warm people, and forced me to drink wine with them. When I eventually returned to the guesthouse. My minders were not amused.

Manekshaw had arranged that we return to India via Rome. At Rome airport, a gentleman drove up in a black Mercedes to meet Manekshaw, and Manekshaw later departed in an Indian Embassy car. I was on the look-out for a taxi to take me to the city when Mrs Manekshaw very kindly offered to drop me off in the city. The Mercedes had come from London and belonged to an Indian businessman. I thanked Mrs Manekshaw and got into the car which dropped me off at Via Veneto from where I took a cab to the *pension* where I was to stay. I had in school read Alex Munthe's book *The Story of San Michele* and was fascinated by it. I went to Anacapri to see his Villa San Michele and was disappointed by its unimpressive appearance, but the blue grotto was indeed beautiful. I also visited Florence and was fascinated by its art treasures.

Thereafter, I spent a few days in London and returned to India. In West Bengal, we were still involved in the anti-Naxalite operations. Meanwhile, in neighbouring Bangladesh there was political turmoil and open hostility to the Pakistani government. In July 1971, I was asked to go to Thailand to see if we could buy some vehicles capable of operating in rice paddies. Brig. F.S.B. Mehta and a colonel from the ordnance corps accompanied me. We tested them and were of the view that they would not meet our requirements. We were also shown the ceramic sandwich armour developed by Prince Tepparit, very similar to the Kanchan armour subsequently developed by the DRDO in India.

In Thailand we met Gen. Kriangsak Chomanan, the commander-in-chief of the Thai army, who I had earlier met in Calcutta. He went out of his way to look after us: we played golf with their top brass and were most lavishly entertained. The ambassador and his staff were envious that we were able to meet a host of people without their good offices, requesting us to get them invitations to the various functions that were organized in our honour. The Thais are a most hospitable and friendly people, and deeply devout Buddhists. I recommended that we send them a large statue of the Buddha, an idea that was accepted and later implemented. The statue today stands in a prominent place in Bangkok.

7

1971: War Clouds Loom

Meanwhile events were moving very rapidly in East Pakistan. The two wings of Pakistan, East and West, differed greatly both ethnically and also in density of population. The 1961 census figures of population showed East Pakistan to include ten million Hindus, and West Pakistan 43,000,000. They differed markedly in language and culture, East Pakistan, the former province of East Bengal, was culturally and linguistically more akin to West Bengal than to the Urdu and Punjabi culture and language of the western wing. The people of East Pakistan resented the dominance of the western wing, most feeling that the western wing was being developed at the expense of the eastern. Resentment against the western wing rose dramatically. In 1966 the announcement of the 'Six Points of Sheikh Mujibur Rehman', the leader of the Awami League, in effect demanded provincial autonomy. In 1967, Mujib and some others were charged with secession, in a trial that was to be known as the Agartala Conspiracy Case. Meanwhile, in Pakistan, Gen. Yahya Khan replaced Gen. Ayub Khan and assumed control of the country.

Elections were held in 1970. Sheikh Mujib's Awami League won 160 of the 162 seats in the east. Zulfiqar Ali Bhutto's Pakistan People's Party won 81 of the 138 seats in the west. Bhutto rejected

Mujib's six points and refused to share power with Mujib. In January 1971 Bhutto went to Dacca in order to work out a deal with Mujib but failed to do so.

Meanwhile, Pakistan secretly began reinforcing its army in the eastern wing via Sri Lanka. On 15 March, Yahya Khan arrived in Dacca to negotiate with Mujib. No agreement was reached and the meeting of the National Assembly was again postponed. Yahya replaced the commander in the east, Lt Gen. Sahibzada Yaqub Khan, who was sympathetic to the people of the east, with the ruthless Lt Gen. Tikka Khan. Incidentally Tikka Khan had been a student in August 1947 at the gunnery staff course I was conducting at the School of Artillery, Deolali before his move to Pakistan in November 1947.Yahya returned to the west leaving Tikka Khan to 'deal with the situation'. Tikka issued orders for a crackdown to start at 0100 on 26 March. Meanwhile Mujib issued a message calling on the people of East Pakistan to resist and drive out the Pakistanis.

Dacca was brought under the control of the army in a matter of hours In the course of an action in which several thousand Bangladeshis were slaughtered. Mujib was arrested in the early hours of 26 March and flown out to Karachi. A number of Bengali leaders escaped. Resistance was fierce, particularly at Dacca University. Meanwhile, in Chittagong, Major Ziaur Rehman took over command of his infantry battalion 8 East Bengal Regiment and seized the radio station. He broadcast from there was a declaration of independence. Major Zia resisted the Pakistan Army and withdrew his battalion to Belonia in the east. Meanwhile elements of the five battalions of the East Bengal Regiment began withdrawing to India.

On 31 March the Indian parliament, shocked by the atrocities committed, passed a resolution calling upon Pakistan to transfer power to the people of East Bengal. Meanwhile, refugees began initially trickling into India, and soon became a flood. In all, some 10 million eventually took refuge in India.

At the beginning of April, I received a telephone call from Gen. Manekshaw telling me that the government required the army to move immediately into East Pakistan. I was momentarily taken aback, although I had expected that we would at some stage be required to move into East Pakistan and had begun planning accordingly. However, to move in immediately was something that I had not expected as we did not have the wherewithal for the conduct of a swift military campaign. I told Manekshaw that we had mountain divisions which were not equipped or trained for riverine warfare. There were several very wide un-bridged rivers we would have to cross and that we lacked the bridging resources for this and had very limited motor transport. Furthermore, with the monsoon due to set in some weeks, the terrain would be virtually impassable. Manekshaw then said that he would get back to me. The next morning he spoke again saying the bureaucrats in Delhi were accusing the army of being cowardly. I retorted that he could tell them that it was the eastern army that was cowardly. He then demanded to know when we would be ready to move in. I replied that provided we got the troops and equipment we required, we could be ready by 15 November, as by then the terrain would have become more amenable. He responded that he would inform government accordingly.

Mrs Gandhi accompanied by Defence Minister Jagjivan Ram, Y.R. Chavan, and Defence Secretary K.B. Lall were briefed in the operations room at army headquarters. I had sent a brief with Brig Adi Sethna, the BGS at HQ Eastern Command. This was read out by General Sam Manekshaw. He turned to Mrs Gandhi, requesting postponement of operations till after 15 November, to which she agreed. Lt Col Sukhjit Singh GSO 1 Operation in the MO Directorate at Army HQ (later brigadier) was present at this meeting. There is no traceable record of any cabinet meeting as Manekshaw claimed.

The refugees continued to pour in. The defence minister, Jagjivan Ram, visited Calcutta but was unable to persuade the Communist – United Front Government to allot land for the refugee camps. The minister requested me to accompany him to attend a cabinet meeting in Writers' Building to persuade the state government to do so. After a long two-hour session the cabinet eventually agreed. Then Jagjivan Ram, an outstanding defence minister, hugged and thanked me profusely.

We were not getting much assistance from the United Front Government to obtain personnel to man the camps. A delegation from the RSS came to see me, volunteering to help; their contribution was invaluable. They also helped our troops to dig trenches. After the war they helped to repatriate the refugees.

A few days later I was visited at my residence by a delegation from the Border Security Force (BSF) headed by its Director General, K. Rustomji, accompanied by Golok Mazumdar (deputy inspector general) and Maj. Gen. Narinder Singh, who was then seconded to the BSF. They were in a jubilant mood. Rustomji then told me that as the army did not wish to throw the Pakistanis out of East Pakistan, the government had asked the BSF to do so. I thought he was joking and laughed. He then replied that the reason why he had come to see me was to invite me to attend the victory parade that he intended to hold in Dacca in couple of weeks or so. I told Rustomji that his forces would be thrown back in a couple of weeks and that he should instead aim to set up bases in the Sunderbans and Chittagong hill tracts. As I expected, about a fortnight later, I received a phone call from the BSF commander from the border post at Bongaon saying his forces had been surrounded a few miles inside East Pakistan. He added that he was about to be attacked by Pakistani tanks and that I should immediately send the army to assist him. I knew there were no tanks in that area, and that his intention was to get the eastern army prematurely involved. I then asked him whether a relief column could reach him, to which he replied in the affirmative. I then told him that if a column could reach him then he could very well return. I told him to fall back with elements of the East Bengal regiments, and that we would cover the final stages of the withdrawal with troops from our side of the border. Some six BSF personnel were captured and paraded by the Pakistanis in Dacca. This was a far cry from the victory parade planned by Rustomji!.

Pakistani artillery began shelling the retreating BSF and East Bengal units. Some shells landed on our side of the border. The acting Bangladesh Prime Minister Tajuddin Ahmed was scheduled to meet a British member of parliament at the customs post on the East Pakistan side of the border. Accompanied by Capt. 'Kaka' Sandhu, GSO 3 Operations of our HQ, I met Tajuddin at the customs post and apprised him of the impending approach of the Pakistan Army. He said he had to remain until the meeting was over. Sandhu and I organized elements of the East Bengal Regiment to provide security for the scheduled meeting. A protective cordon being placed around the customs post. The meeting went off as scheduled and Tajuddin left. We then supervised the withdrawal of the remaining elements of the BSF and East Bengal units. When I went to re-site one of the machine guns an East Bengal soldier laughingly told me that he had no ammunition. I had earlier had 7 Punjab, one of our infantry battalions deployed to cover the withdrawal. When the leading elements of the Pakistani forces approached the post, I directed the unit to stop them from taking over the post and removing the Bangladesh flag which was flying it. They opened fire and prevented the Pakistanis approaching the customs post and the Bangladesh flag continued to fly over the post right up to and after the cessation of hostilities. Despite the initial setback, the BSF played a significant role thereafter in the liberation of Bangladesh. They helped to train the Mukti Bahini; they, together with the CRP worked closely with the army and took part in many operations in peripheral areas right up to the cessation of hostilities. They deserve great credit for their contribution to our victory.

Meanwhile, in early April, a number of Bengali resistance leaders began arriving in Calcutta, prominent amongst them Tajuddin, Nazrul Islam, Mansur Ali, Qamaruzzaman, Col M.A.G. Osmani, and Wing Cmdr Khondkar. A 'Government in Exile' was established and located in a bungalow at 8 Theatre Road, Calcutta. I met with them and discussed a wide range of projections. They wanted to hold a meeting of some of the parliamentarians who had arrived at Baidyanath Tala, which they called Mujibnagar. I advised against this, suggesting that they take the example of Charles de Gaulle and the Free French Government during the Second World War and proclaim a provisional government. Tajuddin asked me to give him a draft declaration. I prepared a short draft and gave it to him, and this was taken to some legal luminaries who expanded it and rewrote it in a legal format. This declaration was eventually issued on 17 April at Baidyanath Tala just within East Pakistan.

I felt that it would be advantageous to get the Bengali elements of the Pakistan Deputy High Commission in Calcutta to join the freedom movement. I asked our Intelligence to make the necessary contacts. This Col Khara did. However, the staff of the Deputy High

Commission wanted to have guarantees for their future service and pensions. I discussed this with Tajuddin and he agreed to their requests. At a meeting with Tajuddin and Rustomji, I told them that it would not be desirable for the army to continue with the operation and that it would be more appropriate for the BSF to do so. This was agreed to and the defection of the Bengali personnel of the Deputy High Commission took place. There was however to be an unfortunate repercussion. Mrs Gandhi learnt of it and congratulated Manekshaw on what the army had engineered. Manekshaw, who made out that he had orchestrated every move, was unaware of these events and screamed at J.S. Aurora for not briefing him. Aurora, who was also unaware of this matter, telephoned me at 10 p.m. demanding an explanation. I told him that this was an intelligence matter and that I had not informed anyone. I told him that if he was not satisfied he could get himself another chief of staff. The following morning I handed over to him a list of the names of officers I thought might be suitable replacements. He took the list and said he would speak to Manekshaw. I began preparing to hand over notes. Some hours later, Aurora entered my office and rather sheepishly told me that I was to stay on. I told him that I would not, under any circumstances, accept being spoken to in the manner he had done the night before. He then walked out. I had no further problems in this regard until the night of 13 December which I will relate later.

Earlier, at the end of March 1971, the Indian government had taken a decision to help the Mukti Bahini. Manekshaw spoke to me, placing me in direct charge of the operation. I got down to organizing camps in the border areas. I visualized a force of some 8000 trainees to be expanded to 20,000 and planned for a training period of some three months for the rank and file and an additional two months for junior leaders. I apprised Army HQ accordingly. After some weeks Manekshaw spoke to me, saying he did not agree with my projections and that he required 100,000 to be trained. I told him that it was beyond the capacity of our camps to train 100,000 guerillas and that it was essential that the training of recruits be thorough. Regarding the method of employment, I suggested that they be infiltrated back into East Pakistan to set up cells there and recruit others for operations. Manekshaw again disagreed. He retorted that three weeks training was sufficient. I responded that our camps were not sausage machines, with young raw recruits going through one end and emerging from the other as a competent guerilla. He responded that as I was incapable of training 100,000 to attack Pakistan fortified posts, he would send a competent general to do so. I waited for the officer who was being appointed to arrive. Meanwhile, Nambiar of the State Bank of India came to see me, asking me for accommodation to set up a bank to finance the equipping of the Mukti. I made available, on a temporary basis, a building in Fort William, which continues to be occupied by them. Maj. Gen. Onkar Singh Kalkat, a member of Manekshaw's inner circle, arrived. I briefed him and allotted him the necessary wherewithal to function. Manekshaw was very interested in the progress of the Mukti Bahini and would telephone on a daily basis to enquire about the number of lungis, rifles, and other items of equipment that were being issued, as also the numbers trained. Maj. Gen. Kalkat was at a loss to answer. Manekshaw then restarted phoning me for updates. I told him that as he had appointed a very capable officer for this task, he should talk to him. He then retorted that Kalkat was incapable of coping and I should answer. I told him that as Kalkat was working directly under the army commander and not me, he should talk to the former. After a short while the army commander entered my room through the interconnecting swing door looking very worried, saying that Manekshaw had spoken to him and made him responsible for overseeing Kalkat and to brief him daily on the progress of equipping as also of details of the operations of the Mukti Bahini. Aurora then told me that as he would have his hands full answering Manekshaw's queries, I could concentrate on planning and organizing the infrastructure, while he would concentrate on the army element of the Mukti Bahini. I was, however, to be responsible directly for the naval and air force components. This was indeed most fortunate for me, leaving me free to get on with operational and logistical planning without interference. The basic layout set up by me continued to function. Major Zia was to be in charge of the Chittagong sector, Major Khalid Musharaf for Comilla, Major Safiullah for Mymensingh, Wing Comdr Bashar for Rangpur, Lt Col Zaman for Rajshahi,

Major Usman for Kushtia and Major Jalil for Khulna. Tiger Siddiqui was to operate from his own area of influence in Tangail.

Maj. Gen. Kalkat was unable to cope with the task assigned to him. He was a good conventional soldier but out of his depth in the environment that then obtained. Manekshaw replaced him with Maj. Gen. 'Jimmy' Sarcar. Sarcar was a soft-spoken Bengali, who spoke fluent Bengali, and unlike Kalkat was tactful and soon established a good rapport with the Mukti Bahini. I for my part continued to discretely oversee the operations.

The seniormost Bengali Pakistan Army officer to defect, Col Osmani, was difficult to deal with. He preferred to concentrate on raising and equipping regular infantry battalions rather than giving priority to the guerrilla-style Mukti Bahini and their operations. I had wanted Osmani and his battalions to be concentrated around Mymensingh to the north of Dacca, to form a firm base for what was in my view the best approach to Dacca. Osmani was opposed to this and I was unable to dissuade him. His home was in the Sylhet area and he preferred to concentrate his battalions there. He got his way and moved his battalions from the north to the east, thus denuding the area of troops that I had visualized as forming the base for the thrust on Dacca.

We were not getting positive coverage in support of the freedom movement from the international press which was sceptical about the reported atrocities. It was essential for us to have a sympathetic and supportive international press, because favourable international opinion was an important prerequisite for the successful pursuit of our mission to liberate Bangladesh from the Pakistani yoke. I asked Brig. Sethna to concentrate on the Indian press while I would handle the foreign press. I briefed Nicholas Tomalin of the *Sunday Times* and helped him with his first piece, which dealt with the atrocities of the Pakistan Army. Tomalin was an outstanding war correspondent who took risks and went into East Pakistan to see things for himself. He was later killed on the Golan Heights, reporting, as always, from the front. Sydney Schanberg from the *New York Times* was another outstanding war correspondent, and was sympathetic to the Bengali freedom struggle. Schanberg later became editor of the *New York Times*. He was involved in events in Cambodia, and his authoritative book, *The Killing Fields,* was a best-seller and later made into a movie. Later, during our advance into East Pakistan, Schanberg walked with our advancing troops from the east all the way to Dacca. There were others too. Allan Hart of the BBC went into East Pakistan and filmed some of the atrocities perpetrated there. We sent in a Granada television team with Gita Mehta (daughter of Orissa politician Biju Patnaik) and Vanya Kewley. The team went in from the east and produced some startling footage. There were other famous correspondents, Tony Clifton of *Newsweek*, Gavin Young of the *Sunday Observer*, and Simon Winchester, among others. I spent a considerable amount of time briefing some of them. The international press correspondents were initially lukewarm in their coverage, but with the passage of time they exposed the atrocities committed. When war broke out the international press was almost entirely supportive of the freedom struggle in Bangladesh. Due credit must be given to these brave correspondents for highlighting the atrocities and thus generating support for the liberation of Bangladesh. Unfortunately our ministers and bureaucrats have yet to learn how to handle the international press much to the detriment of our interests.

Unfortunately, we did not have a proper infrastructure for the conduct of war at the highest level. The chiefs of staff of the army, navy, and air force chair the Chief of Staffs Committee by rotation, their tenure dependant on the remaining period they have to serve, which may in some cases be a few weeks. The chairman has little say in the affairs of the other two services which are autonomous. Much depends on the personalities of the service chiefs, their equation with the defence minister and to a lesser extent with the prime minister. The defence secretary, an officer of the India Administrative Service, has no operational responsibility and is generally not briefed on operational plans. However, the 'babus' in South Block feel that civil control of the armed forces means civil service control. I had to tell them on more than one occasion that they were government servants and not the government, which comprised the elected members of the cabinet.

Unfortunately, the equation between the army and air force chiefs at Service Headquarters was less than cordial. The army and air force chiefs were not on speaking terms. The air chief of staff, Air Chief Marshal P.C. Lall was a competent professional officer. My problem was that I had to deal with two air force command headquarters, one in Shillong and the other in Allahabad, both several hundred miles away. Dealing day to day with one distant Air Force Command HQ was difficult enough, with two, well nigh impossible. I asked Manekshaw to speak to Lall to rationalize this by redrawing the boundaries so that we would only have to deal with one Air Force Command Headquarters. Manekshaw declined, saying that he could not speak to Lall. Fortunately, I was able to meet Lall and apprise him of our difficulties. I also asked him to locate an advanced headquarters of the air force at Fort William in order to facilitate our day-to-day dealings on operational matters, as Shillong was a long way off. Lall said he would examine the matter. A few days later he altered the boundaries so that we only had to deal with one air force command headquarters in Shillong. He also authorized the formation of an advanced headquarters at Fort William commanded by an air commodore. Lall was a very competent, pragmatic officer with vision.

We had very little reliable intelligence of the Pakistani military order of battle and topography. The small-scale maps we had of East Pakistan were over 50 years old and completely out of date. We asked the Mukti Bahini to get us up to date Pakistani maps and they handed over to us complete map coverage of East Pakistan. I took the maps down to the Survey of India's office in Park Street, Calcutta. The Survey of India staff were most helpful and reproduced the maps as they were. We were able to distribute them to all concerned well before the commencement of operations. The Survey of India at Calcutta undertook this project without obtaining the prior sanctions required, and these were subsequently regularized. No lesson seems to have been learnt from this. In 1987 the army went into Sri Lanka without proper maps, and this had an adverse effect on the conduct of operations. Further, for the Sri Lanka operations, Chief of the Army Staff Gen. K. Sunderji advised the government that he would complete his mission in 72 hours! Forces were committed piecemeal and the operation proved to be infructuous.

We began obtaining topographical data with particular emphasis on rivers, tides, bridging sites, ferries, rail and water communication. The corps of engineers branch at the Eastern Command HQ then compiled this data into a topographical manual. We knew little about the ports. Fortunately I had a friend in the shipping business who had earlier worked in Chittagong and Mangla Chalna and got him to brief the director of naval intelligence on the ports and anchorages.

We got very little hard intelligence from the Research and Analysis Wing (RAW), and they actually provided us with just two half sheets of data during the entire period. We therefore had to build up intelligence on the Pakistani order of battle and the location of their units. Pakistani reinforcements to East Pakistan were arriving by air via Sri Lanka and we were unable to identify them. In April and May, I was badgering the director of Military Intelligence (DMI), Maj. Gen. Batra at Army HQ to place the signal intelligence units in the east under our operational control. The DMI maintained that we at eastern army command were not competent to process and evaluate what he called 'raw information', and that he and his staff would pass on to us what they considered to be relevant. So far we had received very little from the Military Intelligence Directorate. His negative approach was frustrating because we could not work without immediate access to signal intercepts. I then spoke to Gen. Manekshaw, promising him that if he placed the units under our command we would give copies of intercepts to the DMI, the navy, and the airforce. Manekshaw agreed and placed the signal intelligence units directly under us. Eastern Command was the only army regional command to have this privilege. We redeployed the units and were not only able to intercept traffic between East and West Pakistan but were able to re-construct the complete order of battle of the Pakistani Army in the east. We were also able to break the Pakistani naval code, that had remained unchanged for months, and to take pre-emptive action. One particular intercept in the later stages of the war was to have serious consequences. The intercept indicated a rendezvous for river craft at Gupta Crossing on the Meghna river. Manekshaw interpreted this to indicate that elements of the Pakistan Army were attempting to flee to Burma. I argued with him that these were not sea-going craft and that in any case there were no sizeable numbers of troops that could be evacuated to Burma. He then ordered Maj. Gen. Inder Gill (director of military operations at Army HQ) to broadcast that he, Manekshaw, knew what they were up to at Gupta Crossing. I requested Gill not to broadcast this message as it would compromise our code-breaking. He, however, was unable to persuade Manekshaw. The broadcast was made and the Pakistan Navy immediately changed their code. Subsequently we were unable to read any further naval wireless traffic.

On 1 December 1971 we intercepted a message from West to East Pakistan regarding a warning to merchant shipping not to enter the Bay of Bengal and restricting civilian aircraft from flying near the Indian borders. We also intercepted signals from the submarine *Ghazi* off Sri Lanka right up to 27 November off Vishakhapatnam. We passed these on the Army Headquarters, the navy, and air force. These intercepts indicated that Pakistan intended to attack India in the course of the next few days. It was perhaps due to this prior information that the Pakistani attacks on our airfields on 3 December were anticipated and therefore only minor damage was inflicted to our air fields and planes.

8

Strategy: What Eventually Worked

Strategy, per se, was not studied in the Indian army. No military institution in India taught the subject, nor was there any strategic planning at Army HQ. However, tactics up to brigade and, to some extent at divisional level, were taught. Tactics may win battles, but it is strategy that wins wars. The Americans won every battle in Vietnam, but they lost that war. The Indian Army's tactics had not changed to any degree from those employed during the Second World War. The army was used to operating astride a road axis with its logistic support following. I had, as a brigade and divisional commander, trained my troops to move along subsidiary dirt tracks, as axes of advance. The objectives that needed to be captured were communication and command and control centres. Towns and fortified areas were to be bypassed and road axes for logistic support were to be opened later. These concepts were forced down on to commanders, who most reluctantly accepted them. There were many occasions later during operations when commanders tried to revert back to metalled roads from their subsidiary axes.

By the end of May 1971 I had prepared a draft outline plan based on the following strategic parameters:

(a) The final objective was to be Dacca, the centre of gravity and the geopolitical and geostrategic heart of East Pakistan.

(b) Pakistani fortified positions and towns were to be bypassed, and thrust lines selected accordingly.
(c) Subsidiary objectives were to be selected in order to secure communication centres as also to destroy command and control centres. Enemy forces bypassed were to be dealt with later.
(d) In order to achieve the above it was essential to draw the Pakistani forces into the towns and border areas leaving Dacca and key areas lightly defended.

In planning any operation for the liberation of Bangladesh, we in eastern command had also to cater for defence against any possible Chinese intervention, contain insurgency in the NE, and in addition ensure the defence of Bhutan.

The terrain in East Pakistan is divided by the Ganges, Brahmaputra, and Meghna river systems into four sectors. We selected subsidiary objectives for each sector. In the north-western sector north of the Ganges and west of the Brahmaputra river we selected the communication centre of Bogra as the principal subsidiary objective. The western sector lies south and west of the Ganges. Critical objectives were Jessore, Magura, and Faridpur (Goalundo Ghat). Faridpur was to be the final subsidiary objective as it lay opposite the city of Dacca. We asked Army HQ for two additional infantry divisions. 9 Infantry and 4 Mountain Divisions were already temporarily located here for anti-Naxalite operations. These we proposed to allot for this sector. The south-eastern sector lay east of the river Meghna. The key objectives were to be Daudkhandi and Chandpur on the river Meghna, an important river port in the proximity to Dacca. We had 57 and 8 Mountain Divisions with no artillery operating in a counter-insurgency role in Mizoram and Nagaland. We could use them in this sector. We would require an additional infantry division. 23 Mountain Division was the reserve for 4 Corps in Assam and could allot this division. For command and control of the sector we could use HQ 4 Corps, whose primary role was to defend against the Chinese in Tibet, which could move to this area leaving behind a small HQ at Tezpur. I had no doubt that Dacca, the geopolitical and geostrategic heart of East Pakistan, was the primary and final objective. No campaign could be complete without its capture. We needed one infantry division plus to move from the north as well as a para-dropped force to capture Dacca. I sent an outline plan based on the above to Army HQ in May which was delivered to the then director, military operations Maj Gen. K.K. Singh by Brig Adi Sethna, the BGS at our HQ Eastern Command. Maj. Gen. K.K. Singh was later relieved by Maj. Gen. Inder Gill as DMO. The monsoon was about to commence in the east. Therefore we had very little time to build up the infrastructure and get the logistics in place. I ordered the brigadier in charge of administration of the HQ, eastern command, Brig. Chajju Ram, to go ahead and build up the infrastructure and logistics to support our draft outline plan. This meant working through the monsoons. We built up the infrastructure to cater for a full corps of two or more infantry divisions in Tripura. This entailed construction and improvement of roads in Tripura, increasing the capacity of the railroad, and construction of landing grounds. A total of some 30,000 tonnes were moved to Tripura. Signal centres and communications were established. Some 7000 tonnes were moved in the north to Tura in the Garo Hills of Meghalaya to support a division plus for the thrust to Dacca. Similarly, in the north-west and west there was a logistic build up. This was done in anticipation of Army HQ accepting our outline plan. We had hoped that there would be no major deviations. As the army commander, Gen. J.S Aurora, was otherwise busy, I did not brief him on the build up of the logistics.

At the beginning of May Brig. Chajju Ram came to me with some routine papers for the army commander's signature. As I was busy, I told him to go directly to the army commander to get them signed. Brig. Chajju Ram told the army commander of the progress in building up the logistical support and Aurora was taken aback and came to my office and told me not to proceed further, stating that we should await the Army HQ's operational instructions. I told him that it was difficult to stop the movement of stores now that the work was in progress. I told him that if we halted the build-up now we would not have the infrastructure and logistics in place when operations did eventually commence. I added that I could not visualize Army HQ making any substantial changes to our outline plan. After much discussion he reluctantly agreed to let the logistical build up continue.

We had at our disposal some military river landing craft at Calcutta and also in Assam, and the Calcutta flotilla had some craft capable of carrying tanks. I had intended to use the Calcutta craft in the Meghna river but they were unable to cross the open sea. I asked Vice Admiral N. Krishnan if his naval landing craft could operate there. He said that because of their draught they could not. I then decided to use these craft in the Ganges in order to support operations towards Dacca from the west. The water level of the Hoogly dropped towards the end of the monsoon so I decided to move the craft upriver north to Farakka in the months of June and July. These craft I had moved on 4 December to Hardinge Bridge which they reached on the 5 December. They reported to the new corps HQ that had been set up for control of the operations of 4 Infantry Division and 9 Infantry Division.

In the first week of August 1971, Gen. Manekshaw, accompanied by the director, military operations, Maj. Gen. K.K. Singh, arrived at Fort William to discuss their draft operation instruction sent to us in the beginning of August. Aurora and I attended the discussions that took place in the operations room. Though much of our draft plan had been incorporated, such as sectors and to some degree troop allocations to sectors, the essential basic strategy and objectives were not included. The aim of the Army HQ Operation Instruction appeared to be limited to taking territory, and setting up a 'provisional Bangladesh government'. The principal objectives were to be the river port of Khulna (the principal anchorages being at Chalna and Mangla downstream) and the port of Chittagong. Dacca was nowhere mentioned. Manekshaw let the DMO do the talking. K.K. Singh stressed the importance of these two ports which he termed the entry ports, and that we should direct our main thrust to Khulna. I was flabbergasted. Aurora, on the contrary, nodded in approval. I explained that the question of 'entry' ports was irrelevant as our navy would certainly blockade them and deny entry or exit from them. In any event, Khulna was only a minor port, the principal anchorages being Mangla/Chalna downstream. Also, although Khulna was relatively close to our border, there were several tidal unbridged rivers in between, with terrain too unsuitable for manoeuvre. Chittagong was peripheral and far from the geostrategic heart, namely Dacca. I maintained that it was imperative that we capture Dacca to control the whole of East Pakistan. Gen. Manekshaw smiled at me, using his favourite term of endearment, 'Jake sweetie, don't you see that if we take Khulna and Chittagong, Dacca will automatically fall. There is therefore no need to take Dacca.' Further heated exchanges took place with the DMO. Eventually Manekshaw turned to Aurora for support, 'Jagjit, don't you agree that if we take Khulna and Chittagong, Dacca will automatically fall.' Aurora replied, 'Yes Sir, I entirely agree.' This was a view Aurora maintained right up to the commencement of hostilities. I was at a complete loss to understand the concept underlying Manekshaw's operational thinking. However, before he left he did make one concession; that he would delete the word 'weight' in the context of the main thrust to Khulna! The meeting ended. On leaving the operations room, Manekshaw put his arm round me and said, 'Jake, I am relying on you'.

There was no suitable machinery for the direction of war at the highest level. Air Chief Marhsal P.C. Lal, in *My Years with the IAF*, writes:

> Here I must clarify one doubt that has existed in my mind and also in the minds of others as to what the objectives of the 1971 war were. As defined by the chiefs of staff and by each respective service chief, it was to gain as much ground as possible in the East to neutralize the Pakistani forces there to the extent we could and to establish a base, as it were, for a possible state in Bangladesh. The possibility that Pakistani forces in East Pakistan would collapse altogether as they did and that Dacca would fall and that the whole would be available to the leaders of the freedom movement in East Pakistan was not considered something that was likely to happen. Caution demanded that people commanding in the east should work to limited objectives but to go about achieving them as rapidly as possible. It was feared that a delay of even two or three weeks would inevitably bring in the UN Security Council and compel the two sides to come to some sort of ceasefire such as in Kashmir. With that basic understanding between the three services, the Army, the Navy, and the Air Force, they were then left to plan their activities as they thought best.

These remarks of P.C. Lal who was known for his professional integrity, clearly indicate that there was no 'clear political aim' nor was there any agreed strategy or coordinated control of operations by the chiefs of staff in Delhi.

We then sent our outline plans to the various army formations to study and war games were then organized at all the formations. Here our strategy of bypassing fortified towns and centres of resistance were discussed. Initially there was much resistance, particularly by the new II Corps (now written as '2 Corps'), who wanted their divisions to advance shoulder to shoulder on a narrow front. During the discussions, opposition also came from Aurora, who had earlier commanded XXXIII Corps and was obsessed with capturing Rangpur and the fortified town of Hilli. Our plan to bypass Hilli was accepted by the corps commander Lt Gen. Mohan Thapan, who also agreed that his final objective was to be the communication centre of Bogra. Aurora was not the only one to be obsessed with the capture of Hilli. Later, on 22 November, prior to the commencement of hostilities, Manekshaw, contrary to my advice and supported by Aurora, ordered us to attack Hilli. Stiff resistance by the Pakistanis resulted in heavy casualties and loss of precious time. There was also much resistance by Lt Gen. Sagat Singh of IV Corps to bypass Comilla and advance on the axis Chaudagram-Laksham-Chandpur. Here again Sagat Singh was obsessed with the capture of Comilla and its Mynamati cantonment. During the operations Sagat Singh diverted troops to capture Mynamati cantonment rather than concentrating on advancing to Meghna river.

Manekshaw was now getting impatient with the progress of Mukti Bahini operations. In September he decided to address divisional and corps commanders in the operations room of Eastern Command. He brought along with him, D.P. Dhar, the prime minister's adviser for Bangladesh and the head of the Research and Analysis Wing (RAW, which dealt with external intelligence). Ramji Kao, who was also close to Mrs Gandhi. Manekshaw then began berating and criticizing the formation commanders on what he termed as their poor performance in expediting Mukti Bahini operations in their sectors. He reminded me of the headmaster of my school scolding his senior form. Manekshaw, based in Delhi, had little feel of the situation on the ground. Formation commanders who had expected the Army Commander Lt. Gen. J.S. Aurora to support them, were at a loss to understand what he had in mind. I tried to intervene but Manekshaw cut me short, telling me that Aurora should answer. The 'pep' talk proved to be counter-productive and was deeply resented by the formation commanders. They had expected Aurora to support them as they had been doing their utmost to produce results under the most difficult conditions. Loyalty is a two-way street, both up and down. The officers present were aghast to see Aurora take the tray from a waiter and serve drinks to D.P. Dhar and Manekshaw.

Aurora did not get on with Mohan Thapan who was commanding XXXIII Corps in north Bengal; they were not on speaking terms. Aurora wanted a cinema to be named after him at the XXXIII Corps Headquarters and Thapan had refused. Another corps commander, GOC IV Corps Lt Gen. Sagat Singh and Aurora initially got on well but relations deteriorated when Aurora learnt that Manekshaw disliked Sagat Singh. Aurora got on well with the II Corps Commander Lt Gen. 'Tappy' Raina, who was a Kashmiri and on good terms with the Kashmiri group of advisers who were close to Mrs Indira Gandhi. Manekshaw disliked the upright and outspoken Maj. Gen. Gurbux Singh Gill, the competent GOC of 101 Communication Zone, which led to Aurora turning hostile towards this officer. Lt Gen. Raina had little or no control over his subordinate Maj. Gen. Dalbir Singh, the GOC of 9 Infantry Division, who openly flouted his orders. Lt Gen. Sagat Singh did not get on with two of his subordinate divisional commanders, Maj. Gen. B.F. Gonsalves and Maj. Gen. R.D. Hira of 57 and 23 Mountain Divisions respectively. These personality clashes had an adverse effect on the passage of orders and their implementation.

At Army HQ relations between Manekshaw and Maj. Gen. K.K. Singh, director of military operations till September 1971, were cordial. K.K. Singh was replaced by Maj. Gen. Inder Gill as acting DMO. Gill was an upright, competent, and outspoken officer, not a 'Yes' man, like others whom Manekshaw liked to have around. Manekshaw wanted to appoint Maj. Gen. Vir Vohra, who was one of his coterie and was at that time attending a course in the UK. Gill did not see eye to eye with Manekshaw on the strategy and objectives spelt out in the operational instruction of Army HQ. He and I discussed the limited objectives and the omission of Dacca as an objective. Gill agreed with me that the primary and final objective had to be Dacca. I asked him to discuss the matter with Manekshaw, and was told that he had failed to convince him, and that Manekshaw had told him that he should study the operational instruction and learn how such a document should be written. Manekshaw appointed Gill as officiating DMO and did not appoint him as DMO until well after the war was over. Gill, who had been a fellow instructor in the staff college when Manekshaw was the commandant, was astounded. He told me that there was no point in pushing the matter further as Manekshaw was convinced that Khulna and Chittagong were the key objectives and that he would work with me to facilitate the capture of Dacca. I told him that as Manekshaw had not allotted troops for Dacca, I would move down three brigades from the forces deployed on our northern border with China. Inder Gill agreed but told me not to reveal this to Manekshaw, who felt that the Chinese would attack us. I told Gill that we had seen no movement on the Tibetan Plateau and our intercepts of Chinese radio traffic did not indicate it. Manekshaw was convinced that the Chinese would attack, a view he held right up to 8 December 1971.

I had to ask for the removal of our chief engineer because he was not producing results. I asked for and had Brig. 'Baba' Bhide posted. Bhide was a 'livewire' with vision and foresight. I told him his primary task was to plan to bridge the various rivers and to make an assessment of our bridging requirements. Our demands for bridging were only released by K.K. Singh in late August and then only after a sarcastic message from me asking whether he was holding on to the bridges for employment in the Rajasthan desert. He released old Second World War bridging in an unserviceable condition, keeping the modern bridges for the western theatre. Bhide, for his part, did a superlative job, not only in having the bridges collected from the various depots but in getting them repaired and made serviceable. Great credit should be given to him for his outstanding contribution in the planning and execution of the bridging operations. When our operations were concluded every single foot of bridging had been laid.

In the beginning of November, we ordered three infantry brigades to be moved down from the mountains to jump off locations for the thrust to Dacca. Inder Gill was put into the picture but Manekshaw not informed. Earlier we had moved down all the 5.5 inch medium guns and the depth artillery units to form the artillery brigades of 8 and 57 Mountain Divisions who had no artillery. I briefed Maj. Gen. Gurbax Singh, the GOC of 101 Communication Zone on the plan to capture Dacca. There was a brigade of four battalions already in position and placed under command of this HQ. Two more brigades from the Chinese border would also be allotted to him in addition to one infantry battalion which was under the command of Brig Sant Singh to support the Mukti Bahini operations. Earlier in October we had prepared an Operation Instruction for a paradrop of a battalion group at Tangail. We had selected Tangail as it was held by Tiger Siddiqui and as such it would be a protected drop. It was the closest to Dacca we could drop and would also ensure a link up from the north.

Plan for the Capture of Dacca

Here I must discuss the plan for the capture of Dacca. As we initially had only had one brigade of four infantry battalions in the north, we planned to move three brigades (of three infantry battalions each) down from the Chinese border. We planned to drop a battalion group at Tangail, selecting Tangail as a safe drop because it was held by Tiger Siddiqui with his force of 20,000. Tangail afforded a suitable jumping off area for the attack on Dacca and was also suitably located for a link up by forces from the north. The operation order for the drop was prepared in mid-October by Air Vice-Marshal Charan Das Guru Devasher, Brig. Mathew Thomas commanding 50 Para Brigade, and me. We planned the drop to take place on D plus 7 and the link up within twenty-four hours. I had earlier briefed the GOC 101 Communication Zone in Fort William on the details of the plan. He was optimistic and told me he would capture Dacca by D plus 10. I sent him a demi-official letter detailing the outline plan as Manekshaw was yet to agree to the employment of brigades from the Chinese border. Both the drop and link up were successfully achieved as planned.

I instructed Capt. Ghosh, signals officer, Signals of 50 Para Brigade to go to Tangail, brief Siddiqui, and ask him to assist with the drop and to move with our troops to Dacca. Ghosh reached Tangail by mid-November and briefed Siddiqui. Meanwhile, Inder

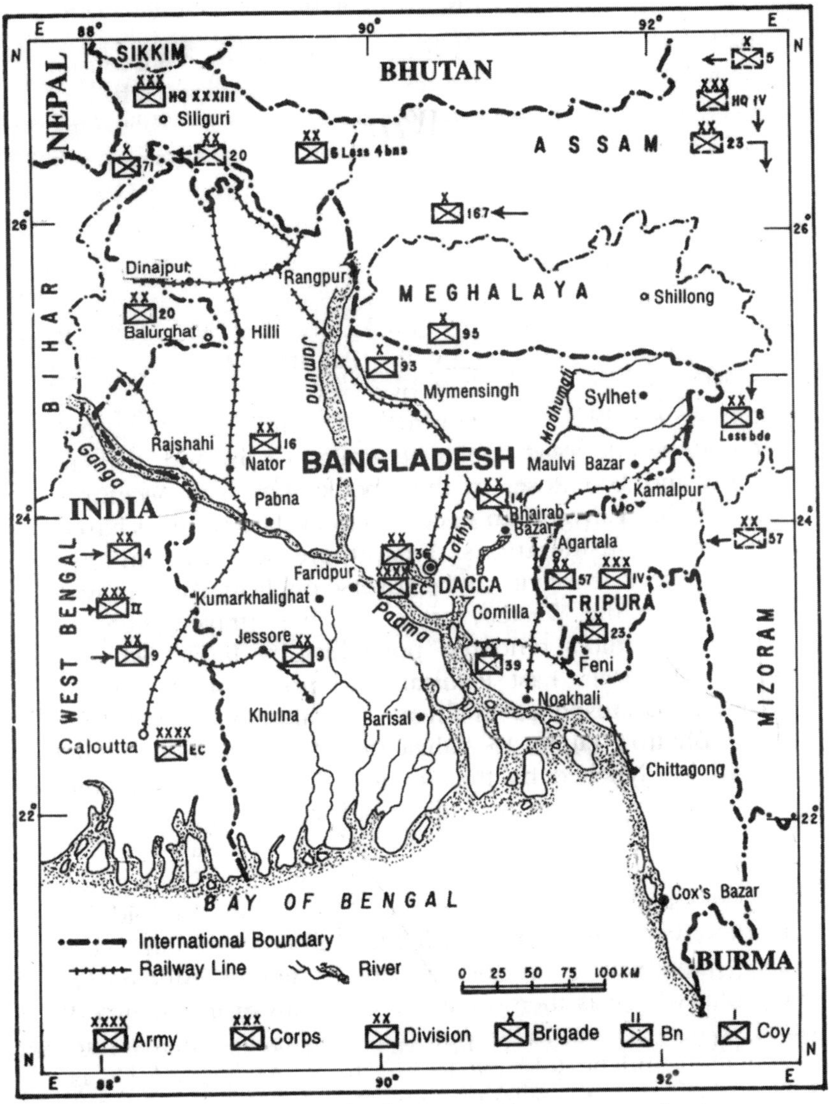

The external boundaries of India depicted in this map are neither correct nor authentic

INITIAL DEPLOYMENT AND MOVES TO CONCENTRATION AREAS

Gill, on receiving the order for the airdrop, asked me to consider the airfield at Kurmitola in Dacca rather than Tangail, and Brig. Mathew Thomas also agreed with his view. I told Gill to remember Crete and the very heavy losses suffered by the Germans. Kurmitola was well defended with air defence batteries. I also reminded him of Arnheim (picturized in the film *A Bridge too Far*) and the inability of the British to link up, stressing that we could not link up with Kurmitola but could at Tangail. In the inter-service operation order issued, Gill included Kurmitola as an alternative. Later Gill said, 'Jake, you were right about Tangail and I was wrong about Kurmitola'. There has been some uninformed criticism by detractors as to why a written order was not issued before the war on the plan to capture Dacca. I wrote a demi-official letter to Gen. Gurbux Gill in November 1971 outlining the plan for the capture of Dacca. Unfortunately all the documents relating to the operation were ordered to be shredded by Aurora. The brigades were moved from the Chinese border prior to the operations but Manekshaw refused to allow us to use these until 8 December, five days after the war began. Maj. Gen. Nagra took assumed command of the troops under HQ 101 Communication Zone a few days before the ceasefire. 95 Brigade Group was already on the move and confirmatory orders were given verbally to Nagra who was moving to join the advancing forces. Nagra had been briefed in detail earlier over the phone by Brig. Adi Sethna, the BGS of Army HQ, and I confirmed the details to him. He also met the previous GOC, Gen. Gurbax Gill, in hospital and was briefed by him. Orders were issued to the other two brigades on 8 December to join 95 Brigade Group to capture Dacca after Manekshaw cleared their employment in East Pakistan only on 8 December, an unnecessary delay of five days. The third brigade, 121 Brigade, had been moved on 6 December from north Bengal to the Western front at the request of the director of military operations, Inder Gill. 50 Para Brigade less a battalion, all air defence units, two regiments of T55 tanks less a squadron, and two artillery regiments of 130 mm guns were also moved to the west on 6 December at the request of Inder Gill as the operations in the Western front were not faring particularly well. I agreed to send them there as western command needed them.

Siddiqui did not fire a single shot at the retreating Pakistanis, nor did he move with his 20,000 men to Dacca. Dacca was planned for in October, the GOC was briefed and was informed of the details through a demi-official letter. There are always 'doubting Thomases' eager to find fault. It was not possible to issue written orders prior to the outbreak of hostilities when Manekshaw only agreed to the employment of the brigades from the Chinese border on 8 December, just five days after the commencement of hostilities. Dacca was a planned operation: the airdrop at Tangail of 95 Brigade Group to be subsequently followed by 167 and 5 Mountain Brigades. One infantry battalion of the Bihar Regiment under Brig. Sant Singh, who were assisting the Mukti Bahini, was also allotted. This was the heaviest concentration on any single axis. Siddiqui with his 20,000 men, who was briefed by Capt. Ghosh to move with our troops to Dacca, did not do so. How can these critics and doubters say that Dacca was not planned for? How could all this have happened without detailed planning? In a fluid battle, it is not always possible to issue written orders, and in such circumstances it is normal practice to issue verbal ones.

Operation 'Jackpot', the code name for Mukti Bahini operations, ended on 30 November. Aurora asked me to brief him on our preparations, which I did. I also told him I had moved the three brigades of our Eastern Command from the Chinese border. I then explained our plan for Dacca. Aurora was taken aback and said that he would inform Manekshaw. I told him not to do so as Manekshaw did not know of their move down and was still convinced that the Chinese would intervene. He told me to draft a signal message for Manekshaw. I reiterated that we should not do so, to which he said that he was aware of what he should do. He then sent a personal signal to Manekshaw. As I had expected, the answer came after two hours and it read, 'I have nursed you better than any woman. Who told you to move these brigades down. You will move them back at once.' Brig. Adi Sethna came in with the message. I told him to take it to Aurora. A few minutes later Aurora came into my office visibly shaken, asking what we should do now. I answered: 'Please do nothing and I will try to sort it out with Inder Gill.' I telephoned Gill who was very upset as he had got a dressing down from Manekshaw for not informing him of the moves. He asked me why we had sent this message as we had agreed to keep it quiet. I explained the circumstances and told him that we all knew that the war was to break out in a few days and if we moved the brigades back we would not be able to use them for our push to Dacca. He said, 'OK Jake, Sam will not agree. I have to carry out his orders. Please therefore do not commit them inside Bangladesh without reference to me, promise?' I said, 'I promise.' I presumed that once the war got underway Manekshaw would agree to their employment. I then again requested the employment of 6 Mountain Division. Gill said that Sam insisted on keeping them in reserve for the defence of Bhutan. It is for the record that Manekshaw only gave permission to employ two of the three brigades on 8 December, five days after the beginning of hostilities; one brigade he had earlier ordered us to move to the western front on 6 December. Despite my repeated requests to Gen. Manekshaw to allow us to employ 6 Mountain Division for the capture of Dacca, Manekshaw refused, insisting that the Chinese were likely to attack Bhutan. This division was therefore kept in reserve and not employed for the thrust to Dacca.

Incidentally, we knew that the Russians were in the process of moving 40 divisions to the Xinjiang and seven divisions to the Manchurian borders. The Chinese were therefore in no position to create problems on our borders as they did in 1965. Manekshaw must have been aware of these moves yet, surprisingly, he did not give any weightage to this information.

Pakistan had reinforced its army in the eastern wing. Lt Gen. Niazi's aim was to defend territory. He fortified the main towns and the approaches to them. In the north-western sector he deployed his 16 Infantry Division under the command of Maj. Gen. Nazar Hussain Shaker with its headquarters at Nator. The division had a reconnaissance and support battalion, a regiment of armour less a squadron, two field regiments, and one heavy mortar battery in addition to its three infantry brigades. Shaker deployed his 23 Infantry Brigade of four battalions in the area of Dinajpur–Rangpur: 205 Infantry Brigade was deployed in the area Hilli Goraghat, 34 Infantry Brigade in Rajashahi-Naogoan, the division also being assigned the offensive task of cutting off the Siliguri corridor and thus cutting off Assam and the North East.

In the western sector Niazi deployed 9 Infantry Division. This division was initially commanded by Maj. Gen. Shaukat Raza who had served under me in the Burma campaign as my battery second-in-command. Shaukat was moved to assume charge as director of military operations at Rawalpindi in October. Shaukat was replaced by Maj. Gen. M.H. Ansari. The division had a squadron of armour, two field regiments, and one heavy mortar battery in addition to its normal complement of three infantry brigades. Its headquarters was located in Jessore together with 107 Infantry Brigade; 57 Infantry Brigade was located in the Jhenida – Jibaannagar area. There were in addition elements at Satkhira.

In the south-eastern sector Niazi deployed the 14 Infantry Division commanded by Maj. Gen. Abdul Majid Quazi. For supporting its infantry brigades, the division had a squadron of armour, two field regiments, and one heavy mortar battery. The headquarters, initially at Dacca, moved to Bhairab Bazaar. 17 Infantry Brigade was deployed in the area Akhaura–Brahaman Baria, 313 Infantry Brigade at Maulvi Bazaar, and 202 Infantry Brigade at Sylhet. The 39 Infantry Division, commanded by Maj. Gen. Raul Rahim Khan, was located in the southern part of the sector with its headquarters at Chandpur, deploying its 117 Infantry Brigade in the area of Mynamati. 53 Infantry Brigade of only two battalions, together with paramilitary elements was based in the Feni area. The 91 Infantry Brigade, a weak brigade consisting of one infantry battalion and paramilitary units was in the Chittagong area.

In the NE, Niazi deployed 36 Infantry Division, and 93 Infantry Brigade in the Jamalpur–Mymensingh area. In addition, each of Niazi's divisions were allotted large numbers of East Pakistan Civil Armed Police (EPCAF), Mujahids, and Razakars. Lt Gen. Niazi's mission was to defend East Pakistan at any cost, and he and his staff assessed that the best course open to him was to defend territory. He believed that if he held the cities and towns which straddled the main road network he would deny us any major ingress. A fortified town is very costly and time-consuming to capture. He therefore held the towns and the approaches to them. In my planning I was convinced that to achieve results, the campaign had to be swift, particularly as the UN Security Council was almost certain to pass resolutions calling for a ceasefire and withdrawal. We therefore planned to bypass the towns using subsidiary trails. Had Niazi concentrated on defending the various river crossing sites and the Dacca triangle we would have found it impossible to capture Dacca.

In early November the vice chief of army staff, Lt Gen. Natha Har Prasad asked me to meet him at Calcutta airport. When he alighted from his air force plane, I drove him to the terminal. He asked me to drive him back to the runway because he had something important to discuss. We did so and I asked my driver to leave the car. The vice chief then said he would not like to discuss matters in the car even if the driver was not present and that we should walk down the runway. After walking down some hundred yards, he stopped, looked around to see if anyone was in sight, and seeing nobody asked me, 'When would you like to have D day'. As the build up was to be completed by 30 November I felt that 5 December would be best as it would allow enough time to cater for any slippages. He agreed and then told me that H hour would be fixed after consulting Air HQ at Delhi. We then devised a code to be sent by Army HQ at Delhi to us. We agreed on the following format: 'Chief of Staff is required to attend meeting at … hours on … December' indicating H hour and D day. Inder Gill, the director of military operations, told me later that Manekshaw had told him to change D day to 4 December as 4 was his 'lucky number'. Fortunately for us, Pakistan bombed our airfields on the west on the evening of 3 December.

Our preparations proceeded apace. The Mukti Bahini too stepped up their operations. From 22 November we ordered our troops to undertake offensive operations into East Pakistan to prepare jumping off areas for the planned operations. The excuse we gave for this offensive action was the need to silence the Pakistani artillery which was shelling some of our border posts. On 22 November Manekshaw ordered that the Mukti Bahini should capture Hilli. Aurora then told me that he would arrange for the Mukti Bahini to do so. I told him there was no requirement for this as he well knew that we were bypassing Hilli. He replied that he would carry out Manekshaw's wishes. The Mukti Bahini was repulsed. Aurora then, against my advice, and also that of the corps commander, decided to commit the regular army. In this unnecessary and protracted operation we suffered many casualties. Hilli was cleared only on 11 December.

American and Chinese moves throughout the period prior to hostilities caused much apprehension at Army HQ. Manekshaw was firmly convinced that the Chinese would intervene in the event of hostilities. I, after studying the intelligence, radio intercepts as also reports from our border observation posts found no signs of any build up in Tibet. Further, in December, most of the passes in the Himalaya would be closed. Conducting operations from the Tibetan plateau would be extremely difficult. The American military attaché at Kathmandu, Col. Melvin Holst, also created confusion in the minds of decision-makers in Delhi by issuing a statement that the Chinese were likely to intervene. Holst had attended with me the same course of instruction at Fort Sill. He called on me in Calcutta after the war and I asked him why he had issued this statement. He was evasive and changed the subject. We were aware of the move of 40 Russian divisions to Xinjiang and seven divisions to the Manchurian border.

The Americans were supportive of the Pakistani position regarding the eastern wing being an inseparable part of Pakistan. Dr Henry Kissinger, the secretary of state, was under an obligation to Pakistan for their arranging Nixon's visit to China as also for making possible a rapprochement between China and the US. Nixon too favoured tilting towards Pakistan, comfortable with the Pakistani military regime and very uncomfortable with Mrs Indira Gandhi who he intensely disliked. On 6 July Dr Kissinger visited Delhi en route to Islamabad, achieving little in Delhi. The Chinese and American support for Pakistan grew, and to counter this Mrs Gandhi turned to the Soviet Union. She sent feelers to Moscow regarding a Treaty of Friendship that had been mooted since 1969 and received a favourable Soviet response. A Treaty of Friendship was signed without compromising either Indian sovereignty or our non-aligned policy and was almost tailor-made to meet our requirements. The core element of the treaty is spelt out in Article IX which states: 'In the event of either being subjected to an attack or threat thereof the high contracting parties shall immediately enter into mutual consultations in order to remove any threat and to take appropriate effective measures to ensure the peace and security of their countries.' This was indeed a masterstroke on Mrs Gandhi's part. It was a deterrent to Chinese intervention and to some extent to that of the US. In view of this and other factors, I was convinced that the Chinese would not intervene. This, I felt, gave us freedom of action to intervene in East Pakistan. Meanwhile, the Ministry of External Affairs sent A.K. Ray, a joint secretary, to Calcutta to interact with the 'provisional Bangladesh government' in Calcutta. Ray was a competent officer and well-acquainted with the current situation. He soon established an excellent rapport with the Bangladesh leadership. His work was not, however, appreciated by D.P. Dhar, the head of the policy planning division in the Ministry of External Affairs. He, together with a very influential group of Kashmiris, pro-Soviet in outlook, formulated our foreign policy. Prominent amongst this group were P.N. Haksar, P.N. Dhar, and 'Tikki' Kaul. D.P. Dhar, when in Calcutta, operated out of the owner's suite at Grand Hotel. I had known D.P. Dhar earlier when I was serving in Kashmir, my meetings with him lasting several hours. He liked to drink English gin and always requested that I bring a bottle with me. He believed that the communists of the Soviet ilk were 'good guys' and that the pro-Chinese Marxists were not. He tried to get me to arm the pro-Soviet communists in the Bangladesh freedom movement. I declined to arm either group, telling him that arming the communists was not in our interests. He totally ignored A.K. Ray whom he disliked, which was most unfortunate. Ray was pragmatic and practical. The last meeting I had with D.P. Dhar was immediately after the Pakistani surrender at the VIP Lounge of Calcutta airport where S.S. Ray, the chief minister of West Bengal, was present. I told D.P. Dhar that it was imperative that we get an agreement from the Bangladesh government on three essentials: firstly, guarantees for the Hindu minority; secondly, rationalization of the enclaves on either side of the border, and thirdly, transit rights by rail and inland waterways through Bangladesh with the use of the facilities of Chittagong port. D.P. Dhar responded smiling, 'Jake you are a soldier. These problems are political. They can be sorted out at the appropriate time.' I responded that the appropriate time was now and that it would be very difficult later to obtain any agreements. He smiled again; the chief minister remained silent. The three essentials requested by me remain unresolved to date. Dhar should have remembered an old axiom: 'Strike when the iron is hot', but failed to do so.

The American position was more complex. Though Kissinger had asserted that he had indicated to India that he felt that autonomy for East Pakistan was inevitable, Nixon on the other hand was determined to tilt towards the Pakistani point of view. Ambassador Kenneth Keating visited me at Fort William in October. We had a long discussion on the situation obtaining in East Pakistan. I briefed him on the refugee influx as also on the atrocities being perpetrated. I told him that I was at a complete loss to understand how the US, the world's most powerful democracy, was supporting such a brutal, repressive military regime that completely disregarded the results of the elections. Keating was a Jew and well aware of the atrocities that Nazi and fascist regimes had perpetrated in Europe in the 1930s and 1940s. He remained silent, disinclined to react, his face a ruddy pink. It was well known that Keating's relations with Nixon on East Pakistan were, to say the least, strained. Nixon's antipathy to Keating and his disregard for his advice are documented in the Kissinger papers which have since been released. Keating's efforts to support the cause of the people of East Pakistan were to be in vain, Nixon continuing to tilt towards Pakistan. Papers released later by the State Department after the assassination of Mujib record Kissinger's instructions to his ambassador and consul general in Calcutta that a 'special eye should be kept on General Jacob', who he feared would march in again into Bangladesh.

Another person I recall with some fondness is George B. Griffin. He was the political officer attached to the US Consulate in Calcutta during those tense months that led up to the 1971 war. Griffin was witness to the entire drama unfolding and though he was sympathetic to the cause of the oppressed people of East Pakistan, he was forced to get into intelligence gathering for his bosses in Washington who had a pro-Pakistan tilt. Tensions were growing between the US embassies in Islamabad and New Delhi. In an interview in 2002, he revealed the role he played and how he befriended Indian military and public officials to get to know the Indian thinking and plans. In this interview he also mentions his visit to my residence one evening when by sheer luck he had the opportunity to study the Indian Army dispositions shown on a map in my bedroom. He of course thought it was a scoop! Little did he realize that it was a set up that I had planned after inviting him to dinner, and there was deliberate false information marked on that map which he was meant to see and report on to his bosses! (*See* appendix for details.)

War

Yahya Khan was getting more and more frustrated with events in East Pakistan, furious at the trans-border operations which had been stepped up from 22 November. He was under great pressure from his armed forces and from Zulfiqar Ali Bhutto to do something. Firstly he was goaded on by the establishment to counter the foreign press reports indicating Pakistan's powerlessness and incapacity to respond to India's 'aggressive' actions, the ruling junta being portrayed as figures of fun; secondly, Indian actions in East Pakistan had not evoked any international condemnation; thirdly, Bhutto taunted Yahya Khan that if he continued doing nothing he would be 'lynched by the people'. On 30 November a decision was taken to wage war on India. D day was to be 2 December, which was later postponed to 3 December. Our signal intercept organization had intercepted transmissions from the west to the east, warning all Pakistani shipping to avoid the Indian coast and also for Pakistani aircraft to avoid flying near the Indian border. These intercepts we passed on to the army, navy, and air headquarters, indicating that offensive action by Pakistan was imminent. It was perhaps because of this prior information that when Pakistani aircraft attacked our airfields in the west no significant damage was caused. Incredibly, Niazi later told me when I was interrogating him after the hostilities, that he had not been informed by Yahya regarding the attacks on our airfields, and that on 3 December he was out of Dacca visiting units in the north. This was confirmed to me later by Clair Hollingsworth of the *Times* (London) that she was with Niazi and informed him of the attack after listening to a BBC radio broadcast. On hearing the news, Niazi returned to Dacca.

At 1800 hours on 3 December I received a call from Gen. Manekshaw informing me of the attack on our airfields in the west and that I was to inform Mrs Gandhi who was staying at Government

House, Calcutta. I asked Manekshaw if we could put our offensive plans into operation, and Manekshaw replied in the affirmative. I informed Aurora of the conversation and suggested to him that as I had a lot of work to do in issuing confirmatory orders and also of coordinating the air effort, he should go and inform Mrs Gandhi.

I got the staff together and dictated confirmatory orders to our formations. I then informed our advance air headquarters that I would be going to the JAOC to coordinate the allocation of the air sorties. I telephoned the three corps commanders, Lt. Generals Tappy Raina, M.L. Thapan, and Sagat Singh, and GOC 101 Area Commander Maj Gen. Gurbax Singh and briefed them. Orders to these formations were issued and the air effort allotted by 2030 hours. Aurora returned at around 2100 hours. I briefed him on the actions taken by me. Our troops were getting impatient and were straining at the leash to launch the offensive. Aurora was in a cheerful mood and asked his ADC, Capt. Mohinder Singh to fetch a bottle of whisky. The whisky arrived and Aurora downed a couple of pegs. I merely took a sip at Aurora's insistence that I drink to our victory. I received a call from Sydney Schanberg of the *New York Times*, asking what action we were taking. I told him that we were having a drink. He asked whether we were anxious, to which I replied that we were confident that we would liberate East Pakistan in a very short period of time. He requested that he be allowed to accompany our troops moving into East Pakistan and I assured him that I would make the necessary arrangements. Sydney Schanberg later entered Dacca with the leading patrols of IV Corps.

Earlier, on the morning of 3 December, Vice Admiral Krishnan, flag officer commanding in chief (FOC-in-C) of our Eastern Naval Command telephoned me to say that some fishermen had found the wreckage of a Pakistani submarine on the approaches to Vishakhapatnam port. We had kept him informed of our wireless intercepts of the movements of *Ghazi*. Admiral Krishnan said that the *Ghazi* had been blown up either on 1 or 2 December while laying mines and that it was an act of God.

I then told him that as the *Ghazi* was no more that should now give him complete freedom of action. The next day he again phoned and asked me whether we had reported the sinking. I answered in the negative, saying that I had presumed that he had done so. He seemed relieved, thanked me, and asked me to forget our previous conversation. Many days later, on 9 December, Eastern Naval Command issued a communiqué stating that ships of the Indian navy had sunk the *Ghazi* on 4 December. Decorations were also awarded to the officers concerned for their part in the 'sinking' of the *Ghazi*. Krishnan later told me that divers had found the log of the *Ghazi,* the last entry being on the 27 November. Divers, who had been sent later to examine the wreck were unanimous that the *Ghazi* had sunk due to an internal explosion. The sinking of the *Ghazi* was announced by the navy only after getting their 'story' collated.

Very recently the Indian media has raked up the issue again (see *Times of India*, 12 May 2010) after discovering there are no official records of what happened to the *Ghazi*. There is little doubt that the Indian Navy did a splendid job, but we did not sink *Ghazi*!

When the war officially broke out on the evening of 3 December, we were well poised for the offensive. As the government had approved our entering East Pakistan up to a depth of ten miles in order to 'silence' Pakistani guns, our formations had moved in November to create jumping-off areas for offensive action. In the western sector, II Corps had advanced several miles and a bridge was constructed across Bhairab river. On 24 November, the Pakistan airforce attacked our troops. We had moved Gnat fighters to Dum Dum airfield. At Command HQ we were in direct touch with the brigade involved and directed our aircraft to intercept. Three aircraft were shot down, two by the air force and one by anti-aircraft fire. I was visiting troops in the area of our incursion and Pakistani tanks were moving in there. My previous experience with anti-tank operations came in handy here. I helped to site our tanks and recoilless guns in anticipation of a counter-attack. Looking through my binoculars I saw an officer, who appeared to be Niazi, lining up a squadron of Chaffee tanks. I watched as the tanks in the tradition of Lord Cardigan's Light Brigade, charged over open ground, followed by the infantry. We let them approach to within 500 yards; I gave the signal to fire and then blasted them. All 14 tanks of the squadron were destroyed and a large number of infantry soldiers killed. I gave a running commentary to Aurora's ADC, Capt. Mohinder Singh who was with Aurora at a party in Command House. The Pakistani tanks were pulled over to our side of the border and were shown later to both Indian and foreign correspondents. The foreign correspondents saw through it but chose not to question the officer briefing them. They were all in favour of our moving in to liberate East Pakistan. The same limited type of operations took place in other sectors. In the north-western sector under XXXIII Corps, the Hilli operations ordered by Manekshaw and implemented by Aurora on 23 November, cost us 67 killed and 90 wounded, the heaviest casualties inflicted on us at any location throughout the war. As we knew of the strength of the defences we had initially decided to bypass Hilli in our planning for the offensive. Hilli eventually fell on 11 December, a totally unnecessary operation which I had opposed, as had Lt Gen. Thapan, the corps commander, and Maj. Gen. Lachhman Singh, the divisional commander (GOC 20 Infantry Division). The other preliminary operations planned for this sector were executed as planned. In the south-eastern sector our preliminary operations were fiercely resisted and some casualties were sustained by us. We were however able to secure the jumping off areas that we required. Thus, on the night of 3 December we were well poised to launch a lightning offensive to liberate East Pakistan. The preliminary operation at Dalai in the Sylhet Sector under IV Corps was poorly executed and we were obliged to replace the brigade commander of the assaulting brigades. We appointed the artillery commander of the division, Brig. Tom Pande, to replace him.

9

The Conduct of Operations

Based on our strategy to go straight for Dacca and bypass centres of resistance, we issued orders to our formations. In the north-western sector under XXXIII Corps, 20 Mountain Division with 340 Mountain Brigade was to capture the communication centre at Bogra, and move up to the Brahmaputra river. The main thrust line was via Pirganj, then down south to Bogra, bypassing Hilli. 6 Mountain Division, which was earmarked for the defence of Bhutan and not at our disposal for the offensive was ordered by us to simulate a threat to the town of Rangpur. The inland waterways flotilla in Assam was moved to the border at Dubri to assist operations down the river. For command and control of operations in the western sector, Army HQ had earlier sanctioned the raising of II Corps headquarters on a reduced static establishment. We had anticipated this and had created the infrastructure, logistics, and communications well before personnel began arriving in mid-November. Lt Gen. T.N. Raina was nominated to command the corps. I had known Raina earlier and had been a fellow cadet and platoon officer at the Officers' Training School at Mhow. As I joined the artillery I was commissioned four months later than Raina and therefore he had become that much my senior. I briefed Raina on his tasks. He was reluctant to take risks and wanted his divisions to advance shoulder to shoulder. He had little control over his divisional commanders, Maj. Gen. Dalbir Singh commanding 9 Infantry Division, openly flouting his orders and frequently being downright rude. The other divisional commander of 4 Mountain Division kept a low profile. We had originally planned for 9 Infantry Division to capture Jessore and then move on to assist 4 Mountain Division which was to capture Jhenida, Magura, Faridpur, and Goalundo Ghat. The inland waterways flotilla was to move down river to Goalundo Ghat to ferry troops to Dacca if necessary. There were acrimonious discussions during the war game held at the corps headquarters. Maj. Gen. Dalbir Singh wanted to move on the main road and not bypass Jessore using the Boyra axis. In order to frustrate this plan he executed a preliminary operation of Boyra, thereby losing the advantage of surprise. Raina too wanted his two divisions to move shoulder to shoulder as he was most apprehensive about his flanks. Throughout the operation Raina was cautious, perhaps over cautious. This approach was responsible for slow progress in this sector. Fortunately some of the brigade commanders displayed dash and initiative.

In the south-eastern sector we had built up the infrastructure for the IV Corps. The corps commander, Lt Gen. Sagat Singh, had an aggressive outlook. He had 8 Mountain Division from Nagaland less one brigade under the command of Maj. Gen. Krishna Rao. The division had no artillery of its own as it had been in a counter-insurgency role. We made up the artillery component by pulling out regiments from the Chinese border. Similarly, 57 Mountain Division from Mizoram commanded by Maj. Gen. B.F. Gonsalves had its artillery component made up to strength. We took a calculated risk in these moves, taking only the director of military operations at Delhi into confidence. The other division of IV Corps was the corps reserve division, 23 Mountain Division commanded by Maj. Gen. R.D. Hira.

We had planned for 57 Mountain Division to contain Comilla and move to the Meghna. Unfortunately we were unaware that the railway line to Coronation bridge had been made motorable. We wanted 23 Mountain Division to bypass Comilla and advance to the river port of Chandpur on the Meghna river. Lt Gen. Sagat Singh was insistent throughout that he capture Comilla and its cantonment at Maynamati. However, given our preliminary operations near Feni, I ordered that the thrust line of 23 Division bypass Comilla and be directed to Chandpur, which I considered to be the more critical objective. We had a contingency plan only for crossing the Meghna river as the navy had declined to operate there. We proposed to allot two squadrons of MI-8 helicopters that we had been promised. As the MI-8s did not arrive we allotted the corps all the 14 MI-4

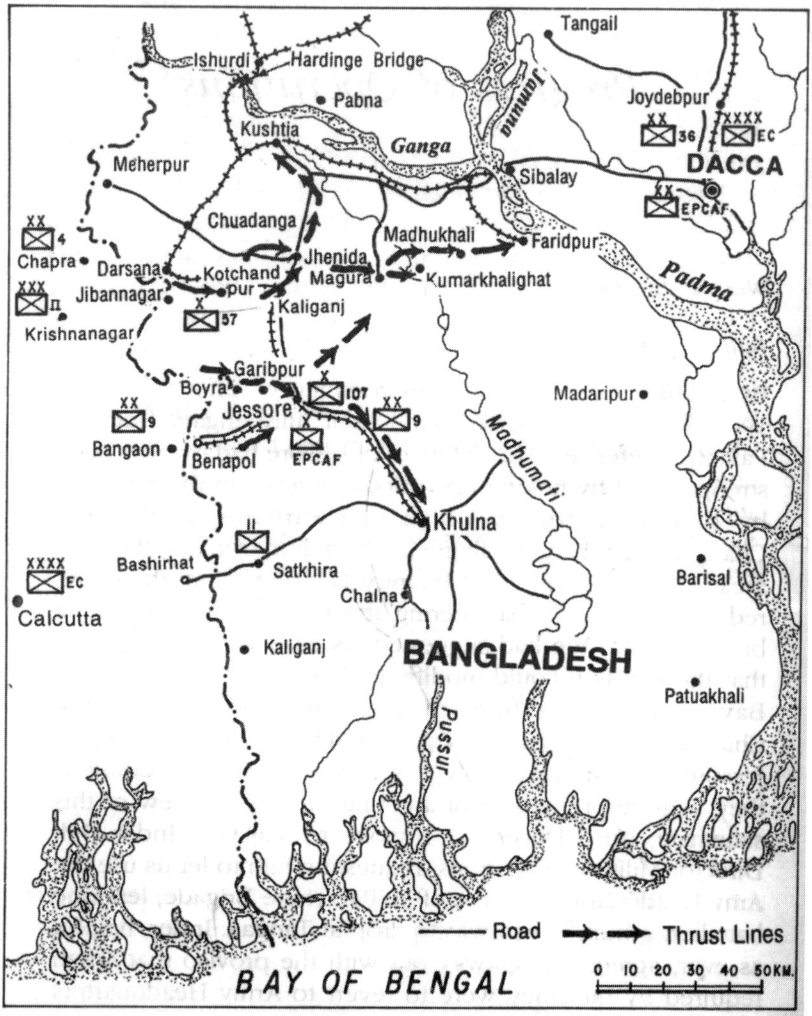

The external boundaries of India depicted in this map are neither correct nor authentic

WESTERN SECTOR

helicopters we had. Though army headquarters had stipulated that the port of Chittagong should be our prime objective we ignored this instruction and gave IV Corps specific orders to thrust towards the Meghna river and, if possible, to cross it in order to exert pressure on Dacca. We therefore had to find other troops to advance to Chittagong. We therefore created 'Kilo' Force to carry out this task. We pulled out the two modified infantry battalions from the Mizo hills (which were organizationally designed only for counter-insurgency), two East Bengal battalions, one BSF battalion, one CRPF battalion, one mountain artillery regiment, one BSF artillery post group, and Mujib Battery. We had planned that Brig Shahbeg Singh with his Mukti Bahini sector headquarters would command this force. I had briefed Aurora who was to visit Agartala to instruct IV Corps and Shahbeg Singh accordingly. Aurora was, however, told by Shahbeg that he would not do so as his military reputation would suffer, and would instead continue with the Mukti Bahini. I was speechless when Aurora informed me of this, and had then had to find a headquarters to command Kilo Force. I then requested the DMO to permit us to use Brig. Anand Saroop and the staff of the counter-insurgency school, which was under Army HQ, for this purpose. Inder Gill, pragmatic as ever, agreed. Shahbeg was very close to Aurora, and after the fall of Dacca worked directly with him in civil affairs and other roles. He acquired notoriety after his retirement when he became a military leader under Jarnail Singh Bhinderwale in Punjab.

I was instructed by Manekshaw that I should also utilize the Special Frontier Force under the command of Maj. Gen. Sujan Singh Uban in our main offensive. I found it difficult to integrate them with our regular forces as I had pulled out the two infantry battalions from Mizoram for Kilo Force. I gave them the task of capturing Rangamati in the Chittagong hill tracts, held by a few commandos and irregulars. The task given was independent of our main forces in a thickly forested hilly area. Their forces moved from Mizoram to their objective. They completed their task by the end of hostilities and then moved down to Chittagong to be transported back to India. Operations in the western (11 Corps) sector were not proceeding as rapidly as we had expected. Initially the Pakistanis resisted fiercely before evacuating Jessore. I kept on prodding Raina to move, but with little success. We were only allotted one battalion group from 50 Parachute Brigade, the remainder of the brigade being

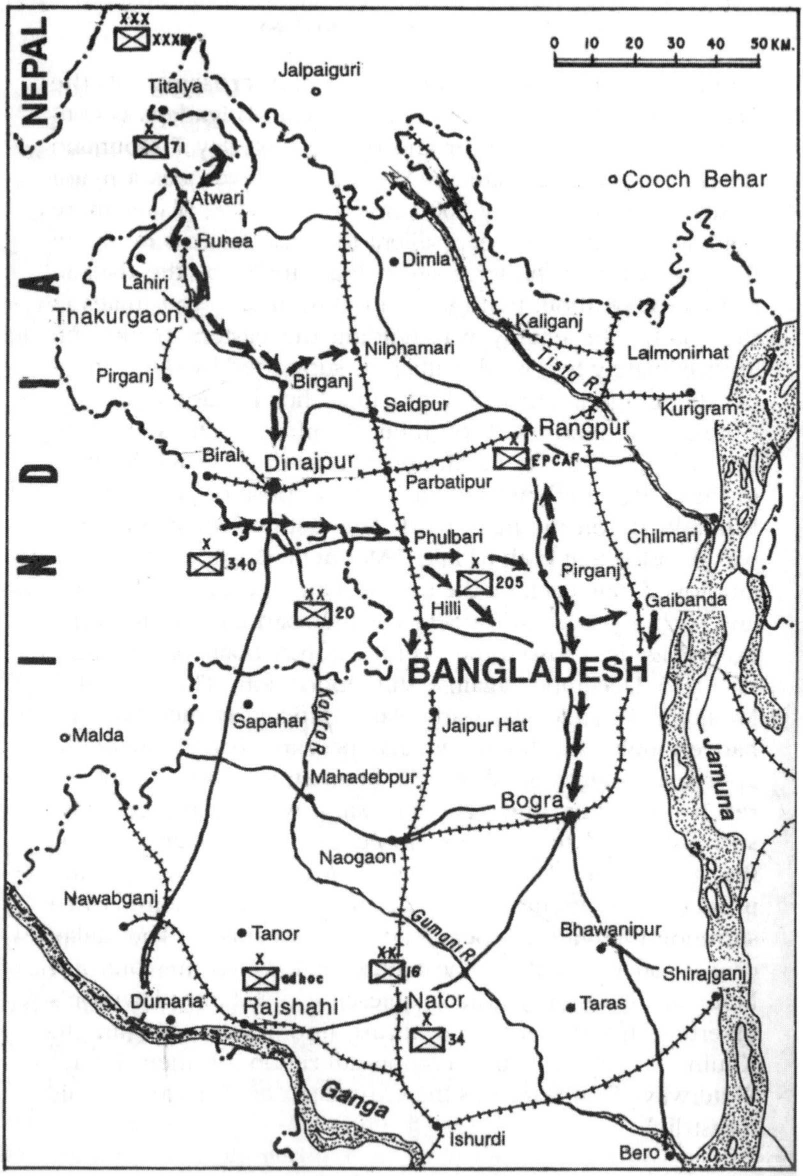

The external boundaries of India depicted in this map are neither correct nor authentic

NORTH-WESTERN SECTOR

held as Army HQ reserve. I then requested Inder Gill to release the remainder of 50 Para Brigade to take Jessore from the rear. After much discussion, Gill agreed, stipulating that it would revert back to Army HQ control as and when he required it. I agreed, and immediately summoned the brigade commander, Brig. Mathew Thomas and briefed him on his mission. I spoke to the corps commander and asked him to give Brig. Thomas every assistance, and if possible allot him an additional battalion. The brigade moved on 6 December. In the meanwhile, Jessore was abandoned by the Pakistanis and 9 Infantry Division moved in. The division was to send two brigades along the Magura–Faridpur axis to reinforce 4 Mountain Division's thrust. 9 Infantry Division spent precious days 'reorganizing', and despite protracted requests failed to reinforce 4 Mountain Division. I then ordered Brig. Thomas to move along the Magura–Faridpur axis. The leading battalion of the brigade met stiff resistance from Pakistani paramilitary forces at Magura. The commanding officer of the battalion, amongst others, was killed in the assault. In the meanwhile, Gill asked me to move 50 Parachute Brigade, less one battalion group earmarked for our para drop at Tangail, back to the west. 9 Infantry Division was given the task of moving one brigade to contain Khulna, and if possible, capture it. The divisional commander decided to concentrate the entire division to this task instead of moving along the Magura–Faridkot axis. The corps commander was apologetic, but took no action. Maj. Gen. Dalbir Singh tried to capture Khulna, committing his troops piecemeal, and in the process sustaining heavy casualties. On 16 December, on my way to Dacca to obtain Niazi's surrender, whilst changing helicopters at Jessore, I was surprised to see an artillery helicopter about to take off to direct artillery fire in support of 9 Infantry Division's belated attack on Khulna! The ceasefire had been in force since the 1700 hours of 15 December. I passed orders to the division to desist from further offensive operations and to implement the ceasefire.

Meanwhile, 4 Mountain Division captured Magura on 8 December and advanced towards Faridpur on the Ganges and proceeded to cross the wide, unbridged Madhumati river. In the meanwhile, a column of 7 Mountain Brigade of this division which had been sent to Kushtia ran into a Pakistani force, was taken by surprise, and suffered casualties. The division, instead of continuing its advance on the thrust line allotted to it, diverted troops to follow the retreating Pakistanis across Hardinge Bridge. The delay caused by the deviation from the original thrust line slowed down the advance to Faridpur. When I spoke to the corps commander I was taken aback by his assertion that he was unaware of this diversion of effort. Not only did the corps headquarters fail to control the advance of 4 Mountain Division, but far more serious was its failure to ensure that the division less a brigade, that was to contain Khulna, failed to move on the thrust line stipulated to assist 4 Mountain Division in its advance to Faridpur on the Ganges. Even more startling was the corps commander's refusal to move the inland waterways flotilla which had reported to the corps short of Hardinge Bridge on 5 December. When I spoke to the corps commander, requiring him to move the craft which had the capacity to move one infantry brigade to Goalundo Ghat opposite Dacca, he replied that he could not do so given the small-arms fire from the north bank of the river. I retorted that I had for eight years on my way to school crossed Hardinge Bridge, and the river was so wide that it was not possible to see the opposite bank. He remained silent and it was clear to me that he had no intention, even if the opportunity presented itself, to use craft for the attack on Dacca. On 18 December the craft finally moved to Dacca to transport Pakistani prisoners to India.

4 Mountain Division's advance was delayed due to the diversion of troops from its thrust line by some three days. 4 Mountain Division, clearing heavy opposition and crossing two more rivers in a series of bold operations, crossed Madhumati river on the night of 14/15 December against determined Pakistani resistance and moved on to Faridpur. It is regrettable that the failure of the corps to control its formations from deviating from the specified thrust lines and to acquiesce to 9 Infantry Divisions not moving on its thrust line and diverting its efforts to Khulna, lost 11 Corps the opportunity of assisting 101 Communication Zone in its capture of Dacca.

In the north-west sector the operations by 20 Mountain Division and 71 Mountain Brigade were executed with vigour. 71 Mountain Brigade moved swiftly from the Siliguri corridor to contact the

Pakistani garrisons at Nulphamari and Dinajpur by 15 December when the ceasefire came into force. 340 Mountain Brigade executed a wide bypassing manouvre of the Hilli defences to Pirganj and then swung south to Bogra which was contacted prior to the ceasefire. The other brigades of Division, 202 and 165, advanced separately in order to control the sector. By the time the ceasefire came into effect, 20 Mountain Division had achieved the objectives allotted to it even though it had to face the fiercest opposition.

In the south-eastern sector, 8 Mountain Division's 59 Mountain Brigade together with 5/5 Gorkha Rifles moving from Shillong successfully contained the Pakistani 202 Brigade at Sylhet, which was needlessly reinforced by 311 Pakistani Brigade at Maulvi Bazaar. We had expected the brigade to fall back to Coronation Bridge on the Meghna crossing. Had they done so, IV Corps' limited crossing of the Meghna would have been very difficult. When I received the intercept regarding the movement of this brigade to reinforce Sylhet I gave a whoop of joy! For all practical purposes two Pakistani brigades were out on a limb, far far away from the centre of gravity, Dacca. After the war, while interrogating the GOC of the division, Maj. Gen. Abdul Majib Quazi, I asked him why he had moved this brigade to Sylhet, to which he replied that he was determined that we should not capture Sylhet. Niazi's fortress strategy and the divisional commander's unimaginative implementation of it speeded up the disintegration of the Pakistani defence posture and speeded up our advance to Dacca.

57 Mountain Division under Maj. Gen. Gonsalves moved speedily to secure its objectives. They discovered that the Pakistanis had removed the rails from the railway line from Akhura to Brahmanbaria, converting it into a road. We had not considered advancing on this axis as we had anticipated that the Pakistani infantry brigade would fall back from Maulvi Bazaar to Brahmanbaria and not, as it did, to Sylhet. We therefore agreed with 57 Mountain Division's request for a change in the thrust line using this axis. 57 Mountain Division, after clearing other resistance, was able to cross the Meghna river with some light infantry elements and send foot patrols towards Dacca. They were unable to get any vehicles or guns across.

Meanwhile, 23 Mountain Division, advancing on the axis Chaudagram – Mudafarganj, bypassing the Lalmai defences, sped on to Chandipur, isolating the garrison at Laksham. Pakistani troops in this area of operations withdrew to the cantonment at Mynamati. IV Corps had by 9 December reached their objectives of Chandpur and Daudkandi, and secured the vital Meghna Bulge. The approaches to Dacca from the east lay open. Later, in Dacca, Niazi told me that when Chandpur fell he knew that the war was lost. I had earlier to push hard to get the corps to accept Chandpur as a prime objective and had orders issued for 23 Mountain Division to advance from Chaudagram to Chandpur against the wishes of the corps commander and army commander who were keen on clearing Lalmai Hills, Comilla, and Maynamati cantonment. The corps, obsessed with Maynamati which we wanted to be contained, insisted in clearing it, tying up two brigades, 61 Brigade of 57 Mountain Division and 181 Mountain Brigade of 23 Mountain Division, with 61 Mountain Brigade being put under command of 23 Mountain Division for this operation. Despite protracted assaults and unnecessary casualties, the Maynamati garrison held out and surrendered only after the ceasefire. Meanwhile, Kilo Force was advancing to Chittagong, clearing Feni on 6 December. Lt Gen. Sagat Singh was determined to get to Chittagong before Kilo Force. He ordered 181 Mountain Brigade of 23 Mountain Division to advance to Chittagong instead of attempting to cross the Meghna. Pakistani forces were preparing defences at Faujdahat on the approaches to Chittagong, out of range of our aircraft. The aircraft from the aircraft carrier *Vikrant* were not available. On the morning of 14 December, two Canberra pilots reported to me for briefing for a bombing attack on Tungi, a few miles north of Dacca. Tungi had been selected by the chiefs of staff at Delhi as a 'strategic target'. Our troops were on its outskirts and it was within artillery range and in the range of our support aircraft so it was by no means a strategic target. I told the pilots that there was no need to attack the target given to them at Tungi, a factory under construction, and of no relevance to our operations and that they should bomb the defences at Faujdahat which was out of range of our support aircraft. I briefed them on the target which they bombed successfully. Late that night, I received a telephone call from a very agitated Devasher, senior staff officer at headquarters, Eastern Air Command, telling me that the air chief had demanded to know who had had the audacity to divert a strategic air strike that had been ordered by the three chiefs of staff at Delhi. I explained to Devasher that we were conducting fluid, fast moving operations and there was no time to observe the niceties of lengthy conventional procedures

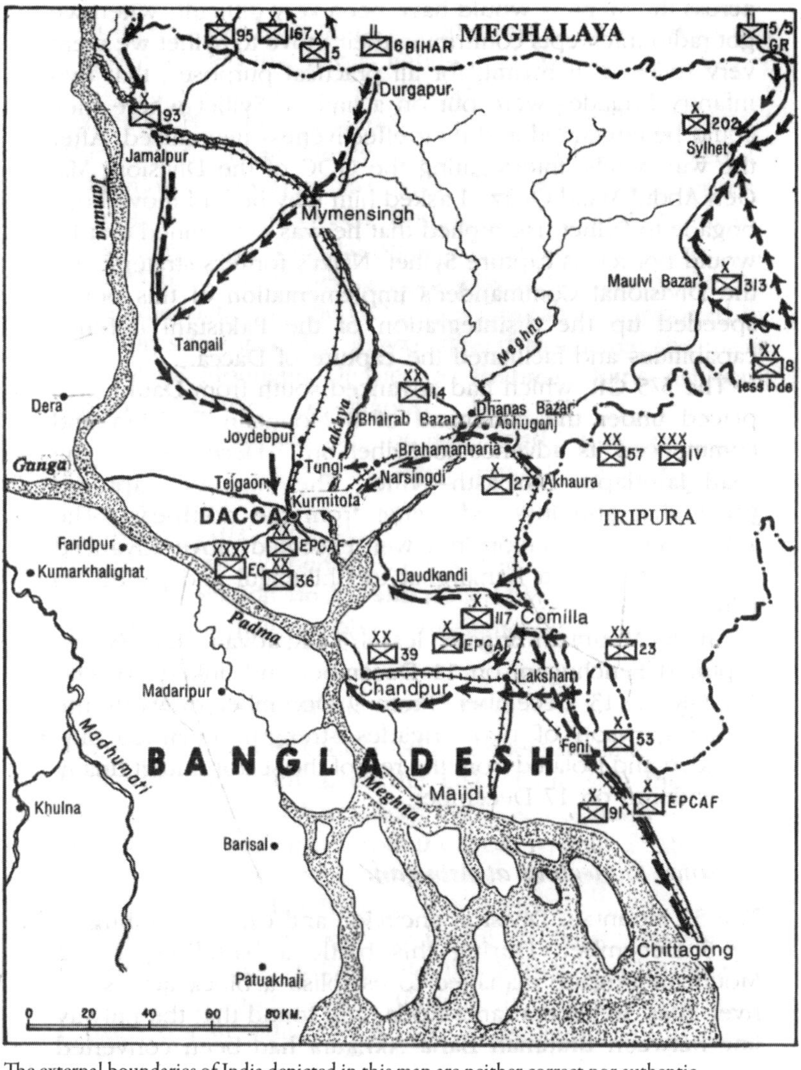

The external boundaries of India depicted in this map are neither correct nor authentic

NORTHERN AND SOUTH-EASTERN SECTORS

of approaching the chiefs of staff in Delhi for their concurrence in a switch of targets. I told him that he could inform the chief of the air staff that the responsibility for this diversion was mine and mine alone; and that the pilots were not to blame. The chief of air staff was a pragmatic officer and accepted the necessity for this diversion and I heard no more of the matter. Faujdahat was contacted by ground troops just prior to the ceasefire on 15 December.

On 8 December Manekshaw telephoned me saying that he could not get the Western Army Commander Lt Gen. Candeth to move sufficiently rapidly and was therefore sacking him. He intended replacing him by 1 Corps Commander Lt Gen. K.K. Singh, and moving Maj. Gen. Harish Rai, Candeth's chief of staff, to command 1 Corps. I was shocked to hear him say that. I knew Candeth well as a good and effective commander. I told Manekshaw that it was inadvisable to change horses midstream, adding that Lt Gen. K.K. Singh's track record in command in 1965 left much to be desired and that the current operations of 1 Corps were pedestrian. After some further exchanges, he said that he would reconsider. I am told that Maj. Gen. Harish Rai, Candeth's chief of staff, in his memoirs has mentioned that he had received a warning order to stand by to replace K.K. Singh. Candeth commanded the western army with competence.

On the morning of 9 December, Manekshaw telephoned me ordering an amphibious assault to be mounted immediately on Cox's Bazaar in order to prevent Pakistani forces escaping to Burma. I told Manekshaw there were hardly any troops that could withdraw along the Arakan Road and, that there was no indication of this. Manekshaw was adamant. I told him that I had taken part in several amphibious assaults along the Burmese coast during the Second World War, and that to carry out such a landing we needed craft, equipment, and troops trained for such an operation. None of these were available. He cut me short, saying that these were his directions on behalf of the chiefs of staff, and that he did not care how but I should carry them out. He added that a team of naval officers would report to me on 10 December for the purpose. I again reminded him that not only was there no craft, but no scrambling nets or life- belts, and that none of our troops had ever been to sea. Manekshaw again repeated that the operation should be mounted and that I would have to find the means to do so. I asked the navy in Calcutta to scout around the Calcutta docks to find a suitable vessel capable of transporting a brigade. Fortunately a merchant ship, *Vishwa Vijay,* had just discharged its cargo, so I gave orders for its requisition. The meeting with the naval officers took place in our operations rooms. None of them had any prior experience of amphibious operations. I had trained for three months for amphibious operations on the beaches south of Cox's Bazaar. Cox's Bazaar itself was unsuitable for an assault landing as a landing there would certainly have been resisted by the small garrison there. Its approaches too were unsuitable for an assault landing. I had trained on beaches around Ukhia, south of Cox's Bazaar, where the beaches were gently sloping and there were some runnels on the approaches. I brought this to the attention of the navy. I told them that I was mustering a force which I was withdrawing from their operations, comprising Headquarters and Mountain Artillery Brigade, which we had earlier allotted to 11 Corps as they had no artillery headquarters, 1/3 Gorkha Rifles, two companies of 11 Bihar, and a detachment of artillery. The navy agreed to provide 150 commandos. As none of our troops had any training whatsoever in amphibious operations and as no special equipment for these operations was available, the naval team agreed to beach the landing craft at low tide and refloat at high tide. The merchant ship with the troops would transfer the troops to landing craft at sea. The aircraft carrier *Vikrant* was to provide air support as the landing beaches were out of range of our support aircraft. The code name given to this operation was 'Romeo'. The force sailed out of Calcutta on 12 December, two days behind schedule, but the very fact that it was able to do so after just three days of receiving orders was indeed a piece of excellent staff work in pulling troops out of combat, and mounting the force with vehicles, guns, and other equipment.

Romeo Force was transferred at sea to *INS Guldar* and *INS Gharial.* So far all the planning had been done off the map, and the actual survey of the beach was yet to be conducted. Unfortunately, the navy decided to change plans while still at sea. Instead of beaching the landing craft and landing the troops dry shod, they decided to disembark the troops by boats and conducted a hurried, incomplete, beach reconnaissance.

Even though I had warned the navy to watch out for runnels, the troops were landed on a runnel. Twelve men were disembarked, two of whom drowned; with another effort, 30 men were put ashore. By that time it was confirmed, as I had earlier advised, that there were no enemies in the area, only a Mukti Bahini camp nearby. With the ceasefire coming into effect at 1700 hours on 15 December, Romeo Force was disembarked between 16 and 18 December with the help of local boats. We were indeed fortunate to have got away so lightly with this ill-conceived operation, lacking in sound military thinking and evaluation. The operation ordered by Manekshaw, based on his assessment that the Pakistani forces were withdrawing to Burma down the Arakan road, was a baseless conjecture not supported by any intelligence. There were besides only very few Pakistani troops in the vicinity that could have withdrawn to Burma. Other than a brief telephone call from Manekshaw, no other orders, written or otherwise, emanated from service headquarters at Delhi. Amphibious operations require specialized equipment and craft, detailed planning, intensive training and rehearsals by the participating personnel of the army, navy, and air force. None of these pre-requisites existed. These specialized operations should not be mounted and launched in the cavalier manner ordered by Manekshaw in the name of the chiefs of staff at Delhi. We were indeed fortunate to get off lightly from this ill-conceived operation. Incidentally, neither the carrier *Vikrant* nor the 150 naval commandos participated in the landing.

Mukti Bahini: A Story of Bravehearts

The organization, role, and the operations of these freedom fighters is well known and well recorded in Bangladesh. However, the role of the Indian Army in organizing the Mukti forces and the conduct of joint operations has not received much publicity in India.

The Mukti Bahini, freedom fighters, Mukti forces, and naval commandos together with the East Bengal battalions played a major role in the operations leading to the surrender of the Pakistani forces in East Pakistan. Due credit must be given to their contribution to the liberation of their country from the Pakistani yoke.

The Pakistani Army's brutal crackdown in Dacca and other areas shocked the people of India. On 25 March 1971 Operation Searchlight was launched in Dacca. Thousands of students were massacred in the university area. The five East Bengal battalions were dispersed earlier by the Pakistan Army. This notwithstanding, they were able to offer resistance. These battalions gradually made their way into India.

On 26 March 1971, the Border Security Force (BSF) was ordered by the Indian government to provide all possible assistance to the revolting Bangladesh forces. The Bangladesh battalions and the BSF withdrew to the Indian border. There was sporadic fighting during their withdrawal. They did, however, manage to destroy a few vital bridges, particularly in the eastern areas. On 29 April 1971, the Government of India ordered the Eastern Army to take over the responsibility of assisting the Bangladesh forces in their struggle to liberate their country. The BSF located in the theatre were placed under the operational command of the Eastern Army.

Meanwhile, by the end of March 1971, Bangladesh resistance leaders began arriving in Calcutta. Prominent among these was Tajuddin Ahmed, Nazrul Islam, Qamaruzzaman, Mansur Ali, Col. Mag. Osmani and Wing Commander Khandker. A government in exile was soon formed and housed in a bungalow at 8 Theatre Road. I helped in setting up the infrastructure for both headquarters. I attended some cabinet meetings and frequently met Osmani and Khandker.

Army HQ spelt our three tasks for Eastern Command. The first was to advise and guide the provisional government of Independent East Bengal in their endeavour to wage a campaign of guerilla warfare in East Pakistan.

The next task given was to organize and equip a guerilla force of some 20,000 which could subsequently be expanded to 1,00,000. Eastern Command was to plan, direct, and coordinate guerilla operations in East Pakistan. The guerillas were in the initial stages to operate where there were no Pakistani forces. This was to be followed by striking at outposts, convoys, and sabotage. Finally, the guerillas were to operate as sub-units and groups. I disagreed with the concept of the numbers to be trained and their employment. Manekshaw insisted that 1,00,000 were to be trained. Once trained, they should be employed to attack fortified Pakistani defences. I told him that we had begun setting up eight camps each with the capacity to train 1,000 plus at any one time. I required a period of some three months to train the guerillas and some five months to train junior leaders. Manekshaw replied that three to four weeks were sufficient. I responded that our camps were not sausage machines through one end of which a recruit entered and three weeks later emerged from the other side as a guerilla. He then said that if I could not produce 1,00,000 trained fighters he would send someone who could. Maj. Gen. Onkar Singh Kalkar arrived in May but was unable to cope. Manekshaw then phoned me, saying that Kalkar was unable to respond to his queries, and that I should do so. I told him he should ask the army commander. He then retorted that Aurora was unable to do so. I then oversaw the training and operations; I was told by Aurora that he would handle the training and equipping of the freedom fighters and that I should look after the naval and air wings, and also coordinate the operations of the freedom fighters.

A senior officer of the State Bank of India, a certain Mr Nambiar, was nominated as financial adviser, and asked for a suitable building. This was given and never returned. Today, it still houses the Fort William branch of the State Bank of India.

The Bangladesh Forces HQ was set up at 8 Theatre Road along with the provisional government of Bangladesh. Col. Osmani, in consultation with the Eastern Command, divided the theatre of operations into 8 sectors. Each sector had a Bangladeshi office with a small staff. They worked in conjunction with Indian Army sector commanders in operation 'Jackpot', the code name for the operations of the Bangladesh forces.

Major Zia was to be responsible for the Chittagong sector, Major Khalid Musharaf for Comilla, Major Saifullah for Mymensingh, Wing Commander Bashar for Rangpur, Lt Col Zaman for Rajshahi, Major Usman for Kushtia, and Major Jalil for Khulna. 'Tiger' Siddiqui decided to operate on his own from the area he controlled in Tangail, as did Noorul Kadar and Toha. The Indian Army formation commanders in which the sectors were located provided guidance.

We had set up the training camps with a capacity of some 1000 plus trainees. Moorti Camp, A sector in north Bengal, was to be run by 20 Mountain Division as was the Raiganj camp in B Sector. 9

Infantry Division was to run Chakulya Camp in C Sector. Deotamura Camp in Tripula, D Sector was to be run by 57 Mountain Division as was Masimpur in E Sector in Assam. Tura Camp, Sector F.J. in Meghalaya was to be run by 101 Communication Zone. The camp at Silchar in E Sector was to be run by 8 Mountain Division and Dauki, E Sector by 101 Communication Zone.

A total of some 80,000 freedom fighters were organized into teams of 10, squads of 20, and groups of 100. They were armed with rifles, grenades, light machine guns, and explosives. To provide junior leaders of the regular battalions, some 130 cadets were trained at Moorti Camp. Some of those who were trained there visited the camp in 2010.

I was assigned the specific task of training and planning the operations of the naval commandos. The navy assigned Commander Mathis, a live-wire, to assist me. Some 400 naval commandos were trained in the upper reaches of the river Hoogly. I negotiated with the West Bengal Government to loan me two sea-going craft, the *Padma* and *Pallas*. We had 40 mm L 60 air-defence guns mounted on them. The navy also assigned a submariner, Commander Samant, to assist me. Both Mathis and Samant reported directly to me.

I had, as I mentioned earlier, serious differences with Osmani with regard to priorities. I wanted the maximum effort to be placed on the training and equipping of the Mukti forces. Osmani had a typical regular army officer`s reservation regarding irregular forces and wanted to focus on raising more regular units rather than concentrating on the freedom fighters. Khandker, however, agreed with my views. Osmani, despite my objections raised three more regular battalions, the personnel being taken from the freedom fighters we had trained.

The five regular East Bengal battalions were reorganized and equipped. 1, 3, and, 7 East Bengal were moved to Tura in Meghalaya and placed under a brigade headquarters and named Z Force. 2 and 4 East Bengal were located in Tripura and re-equipped there. In addition to the East Bengal battalions, three artillery batteries were raised. The Bangladesh regular forces were divided into three forces: *Z Force* comprised 1, 3, 8 East Bengal supported by No. 2 Field Battery, *K Force* consisted of 10 and 11 East Bengal supported by

No. 3 Battery. *S Force* comprised 2, 4, and 9 East Bengal supported by No. 1 Battery (Mujib).

Our Air Force transferred to the air component of the Bangladesh Air Force one Otter, one Dakota, and one Aloutte helicopter. The air component also operated directly under me.

From August 1971, freedom fighters were infiltrated into East Pakistan. Initially a few hundred were infiltrated and by the end of November, some 50,000 freedom fighters had been infiltrated. They attacked and harassed the Pakistani armed forces as well as the paramilitary. They instilled a feeling of fear into the rank and file of the Pakistani Army, their operations having a devastating effect on the morale of the Pakistan armed forces. The freedom fighters also gained control of some areas inside East Pakistan. Tiger Siddiqui, with some 20,000 of his followers, controlled Tangail; Zia controlled areas in the east.

The freedom fighters destroyed and disrupted the infrastructure, lines of communication, and logistics of the Pakistan Army. They blew up bridges and railway tracks causing railway traffic to come to a standstill. They blew up power pylons interrupting power supply. They created an environment of fear throughout the rank and file of Pakistani Army and therefore their contribution to the defeat of the Pakistani armed forces was enormous and their achievements should be given due credit.

Some 400 naval commandos and frogmen were trained under Commander Mathis of the Indian Navy, seconded to us at Plassey at the scene of the battle between Siraj-ud-Daula and Robert Clive. The mango groves are still there. With help from a Mukti gunboat mounting a Bofors L60 40mm gun, they captured, sank, and damaged some 15 Pakistani ships, 11 coastal vessels, 7 gunboats, 11 barges, 2 tankers, and 19 river craft. Their achievements were most significant.

We wanted to give the Mukti Navy some more craft. I talked to Calcutta Port Commissioners, and then the chief minister, who were all most helpful. They agreed to loan us two craft, the *MV Palash* and *MV Padma*. We reinforced their decks and mounted Bofors L60, 40mm guns on them. The craft were manned by Bangladeshi personnel formely of the Pakistan Navy. Commander Samant, the submariner seconded to us by the Indian Navy was placed by me to command the *Padma* and *Palash*. Commanders Mathis and Samant operated directly under me and not Eastern Naval Command. The two craft played havoc on shipping approaching East Pakistan. I recall one evening sitting at the residence of a friend of mine in the shipping business I was shown by the captain of a foreign ship some unexploded 40mm shells which bore Indian marking which he said were fired at his ship. I told him that they were most probably fired by Pakistani craft and I could not understand from where they had obtained the ammunition!

I ordered Samant to attack Pakistani shipping in the anchorages of Chalna and Mangla, and that he was not to go beyond the two anchorages as our troops were in contact with Khulna. I tied up with Advance Air HQ at Fort William and fixed the bomb-line. The Air Force asked me to have the decks of the two craft painted yellow for recognition. I briefed Samant on his task, on the bomb-line, which he should not cross and instructed him to paint the decks yellow.

The *Padma* and *Palash* had considerable success en route, sinking many craft on the night of 9/10 December. Samant and his task force of *Padma* and *Palash* entered the anchorage of Mangla. Samant in his over-eagerness decided to attack Khulna. He sailed past the bomb line, our aircraft failed to identify the yellow painted decks, and attacked and sank both craft. Samant and the crews of both craft managed to swim ashore. Mukti Bahini were in control of the area, and arranged for their return. We were most impressed by the guts Samant displayed and put his name up for a Mahavir Chakra, which he duly received.

The West Bengal government sought compensation for the loss of the *Padma* and *Palash*. Our financial advisor agreed to reimburse the depreciated cost of the craft. The state government, however, wanted the amount required to buy two new craft. I persuaded the financial advisor that in view of the unstinted help provided to our armed forces prior to and during the operations, we should provide sufficient money for two new craft. The latter agreed, and I was thanked by the chief minister for this.

For guerilla operations to succeed, they must strike deep into the roots of the enemy. To achieve success, time, organization, and motivation are important. No guerilla operation can produce quick results. We had a limited time-frame, from May to November 1971, within which we had to train and equip a guerilla force.

The untrained individuals enrolled by the Mukti Bahini had little knowledge of small arms and explosives. I had pressed Manekshaw to give them three months training but was overruled. The young recruits were given between three and four weeks training, barely adequate to train a guerilla. Junior leaders required at least five to six months training. We tried to ensure this. This lack of an adequate training period was to limit their effectiveness. The selection of trainees was somewhat haphazard and the lack of sufficient trained junior leaders severely restricted the conduct of operations.

Osmani, as mentioned earlier, was unfortunately not overly keen on guerilla operations, preferring to concentrate on raising of regular battalions. He withdrew three of the five regular battalions from preliminary operations and formed them into a brigade. Later he raised three more battalions and two more brigade headquarters. The personnel for these raisings were taken from the ranks of the freedom fighters, thus reducing the numbers available for guerilla operations. The regular battalions took part in November and December in some well-executed operations. As we were unable to spare regular Indian Army troops to capture Chittagong, the primary objective spelt out by Manekshaw, a mixed force of East Bengal battalions with two modified infantry battalions was ordered to advance to Chittagong. They reached the outskirts of the city when the ceasefire came into force on 15 December.

The conduct of guerilla operations is complex. These operations, to succeed, need careful planning, thorough briefing, carefully planned induction, and effective command and control. The sector headquarters of the Mukti Bahini were insufficiently staffed and were not able to plan and control operations to the required standards. The induction of guerillas was not properly organized, the targets assigned were too ambitious, and at times haphazard. On occasions when they were confronted with stiff opposition they gravitated back to the Indian border. Sometimes they lacked motivation. For example, 'Tiger Siddiqui', though he helped to retrieve stores from the air drop at Tangail, did nothing to intercept the Pakistan

Parents: Elias and Carrie Jacob, 1917.

Jack (extreme right) with father and brothers, 1930.

Young Jack (extreme left) with brothers Maurice and Eric, 1938.

At school in Darjeeling, 1938.

1939 N.B.M.R. (Northern Bengal Mounted Rifles): BAKER SHIELD
JFR (seated left corner) with the Baker Shield..

As Second Lieutenant prior to embarking for the Middle East, 1942.

Carrying the Commander-in-Chief's banner, 1942.

Officer Cadet JFR Jacob in Mhow, 1942.

JFR (in front) Crossing the Nastachun Pass, Kupwara, Jammu & Kashmir, 1952.

JFR (right) with his charger, Patiala Battery, 1953.

JFR (right) with Second Lieutenant Tony D'Silva, 75 Patiala Mountain Battery, 1953.

New Year's Party: Armoured Division Artillery Mess, 1954. JFR on extreme right with pipe.

JFR (fourth from right) with officers of 3 Field Regiment, Officers' Mess, 1956.

With his Labrador, Jodhpur, 1969.

With monks in Ladhak.

A bridge across Gorai-Madhumati river, East Pakistan, 1971, constructed by the Indian Armed Forces. *Photo courtesy: United Services Institute, New Delhi.*

Surrender at Dacca, 16 December 1971. JFR is standing on extreme right.

Mukti Forces, East Pakistan, 1971. *Photo courtesy: United Services Institute, New Delhi.*

Field Marshal Roberts, Bengal Artillery statue at the entrance of Artillery Centre, Nashik.

Indian tanks advancing in the Jhenida sector, East Pakistan, 1971. *Photo courtesy: United Services Institute, New Delhi.*

With Pal Singh Gill on the banks of River Rawi, 1972.

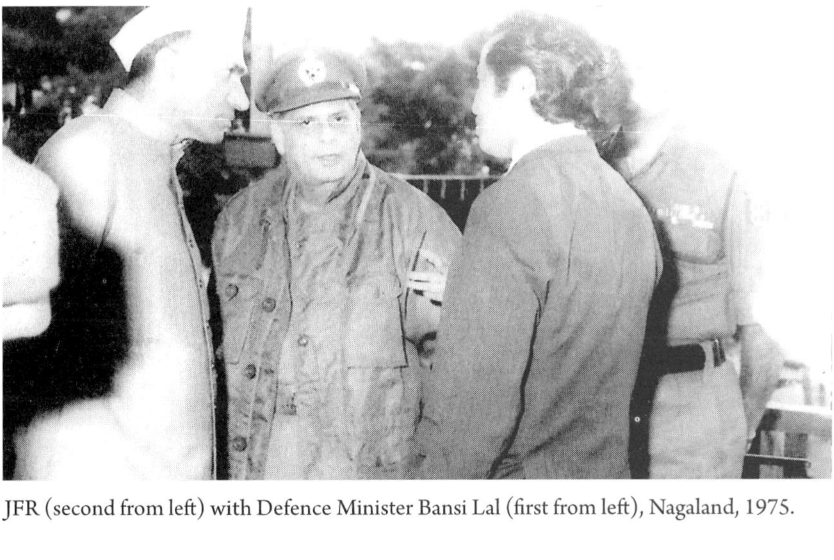

JFR (second from left) with Defence Minister Bansi Lal (first from left), Nagaland, 1975.

With filmstar
Praveen Babi,
Calcutta, 1975.

JFR with Gen Abbassi (centre), Commander-in-Chief Iranian Army and his wife, Calcutta, 1977.

JFR with Jyoti Basu, Chief Minister West Bengal, 1977.

JFR (second from right) with Iraqi military delegation headed by Maj. Gen. Najdat Kassim Maksoud, Fort William, Calcutta, 1979.

JFR (extreme right) with Queen of England, Queen Elizabeth II.

JFR with Patiala Mountain Battery.

JFR at the inauguration ceremony as Governor of Goa, 1999.

JFR receiving Honorary Doctorate, Punjab University from Vice President Bhairon Singh Shekhawat, Chandigarh, 2003.

Jacob family benches at Bethel Synagogue, Calcutta.

JFR with President of Israel, Shimon Peres, 2008.

forces withdrawing from Jamalpur and Mymensingh through his stronghold at Tangail. I had also requested the freedom fighters to organize a Second World War French Maquis type of uprising in Dacca. This also did not materialize.

Due credit must, however, be given to the achievements of the Mukti Bahini and the East Bengal battalions. They played a crucial and major role in the operations leading to the surrender of the Pakistan Eastern Command. They fought with courage and determination notwithstanding the limitations of inadequate training and lack of sufficient junior leaders. They created an environment of fear for the Pakistan Army and completely demoralized them, restricting their ability to move and virtually confining them to their posts and defences. They demoralized the Pakistani forces and eroded their will to fight. They occupied large areas of territory, demolishing bridges, electric pylons, and harassing the Pakistanis wherever they could.

For many years both India and Bangladesh played down the contributions of both countries to the defeat of the Pakistani Eastern Command. However, in March 2008, the Bangladesh Army invited ten officers and their wives from India. I led the delegation. The visit lasted ten days, and during it the red carpet was laid out for us and we were royally feted. The Press covered our visit in glowing terms. Delegations from Bangladesh attend Vijay Diwas celebrations on the 16 December at Fort William. Both armies now give due importance to the joint efforts of the Eastern Army, the East Bengal battalions, the freedom fighters, and the people of Bangladesh who made victory possible.

10

Surrender: The True Story

The airdrop on 11 December at Tangail, planned in October, was a complete success. The link-up with troops from the north took place, as planned, on 12 December. The troops reached the outskirts of Dacca on 13 December. Siddiqui and his 20,000 men failed to move with our troops to Dacca.

There was hectic activity at the UN. The Soviets had thus far vetoed all resolutions that did not link a ceasefire with the recognition of the will of the people of East Pakistan.

On 6 December George Bush, the American ambassador at the UN, called for an immediate ceasefire and withdrawal of our troops. This resolution too was vetoed by the Soviet Union. An Argentine resolution in the General Assembly demanding a ceasefire and withdrawal of our troops was passed by 104 votes to 11.

Consternation was caused in Delhi by the movement of the American aircraft carrier *Enterprise*, an amphibious assault ship, four guided missile destroyers, a guided missile frigate, and landing craft. It moved through the Straits of Malacca on the night of 13/14 December. The task force moved into the Indian Ocean through the great channel between Sumatra and the Great Nicobar with the Indian Navy wholly unaware that any such movement was taking place.

On 13 December there was an American resolution in the Security Council demanding an immediate withdrawal which was vetoed by the Soviet Union. The latter then informed us that there would be no more vetoes. Manekshaw then issued an order to us to capture all the towns we had bypassed, and cited these. There was no mention at all of Dacca though we were on the outskirts. He copied this order to our corps commanders. If we implemented this order we would have had to pull back our troops. At the Eastern Command, we decided to ignore it and proceed with our offensive on Dacca! I am reminded of a parallel: Nelson prior to battle of Copenhagen in 1801, when ordered to withdraw, put the telescope to his blind eye with words, 'I see no order to withdraw: Attack!!'

I was being blamed for the strategy and plan to bypass the towns and go for Dacca. I was told by Aurora that 'my head would be on the chopping block'. I got through to Niazi on the wireless on the night of 13 December, and offered generous terms if he surrendered; that we would ensure protection of ethnic minorities and that the forces who surrendered would be treated with the dignity due to soldiers as required by the Geneva Convention. I also spoke to him on 14, 15, and the morning of 16 December.

On the morning of 14 December we got a lucky break: a signal intercept indicating that there was to be a meeting at Government House at 1200 hours. We arranged with the air force to bomb it. The strike was effective and the governor, Dr Abdul Motaleb Malik resigned and went to the Intercontinental Hotel. That was the end of the last government of East Pakistan. That evening Niazi and Farman Ali handed over a ceasefire proposal to the American Consul General Spivack, the proposal specifying:

(1) A ceasefire and a cessation of all hostilities,
(2) hand-over of the administration to the UN,
(3) the UN ensuring
    (a) the safety of all armed and paramilitary forces pending their return to West Pakistan.
    (b) the safety of all West Pakistan civilians,
    (c) the safety of all migrants settled since 1947,
    (d) no reprisals.

There was no mention of India in the proposals.

The message was delievered to Bhutto in New York on 15 December where he was attending meetings of the Security Council. Bhutto rejected the ceasefire proposals outright. The Security Council that night was debating a Polish Resolution (Soviet block) requiring a ceasefire and withdrawal. Bhutto tore up the resolution as it did not, as other resolutions, condemn India for being an aggressor. He shouted at the meeting that they would never surrender but would fight to the bitter end.

On the morning of 16 December, Manekshaw phoned me and said, 'Jake, go and get a surrender'. I asked him if I should negotiate the surrender on the basis of the draft sent to him some days earlier. He replied, 'You know what to do; just go'. I then mentioned that Niazi had invited me for lunch, and informed Aurora. I met Mrs Bhanti Aurora outside the office, and she told me that she was going to Dacca as her place was beside her husband. I returned to Aurora and asked him if he was taking his wife with him. He replied in the affirmative. I said it was risky taking her there, to which he replied that it would be my responsibility to ensure her safety!

I proceeded to Dacca accompanied by a staff officer. I took my draft of the Instrument of Surrender, which was yet to be confirmed by Army HQ. I changed helicopters at Jessore to save refuelling time. An officer ran up to me handing over a signal message from Army HQ. I expected that the message would confirm the draft I was carrying with me. It read: 'Government of India has approved of General Jacob having lunch with Gen. Niazi.' I proceeded on to Dacca.

On landing at Dacca, I was met by the representatives of the UN, Marc Henry, Kelly, and others. They told me that they were accompanying me to take over the government and to arrange the withdrawal of the Pakistan military, paramilitary, and Pakistani civilians. I thanked them but declined their offer. Fighting was going on in Dacca between the Mukti Bahini and the Pakistan Army.

The Pakistanis had sent me a staff car. The chief of staff of Pakistan's Eastern Command accompanied me in the car to the headquarters of Eastern Command. We had barely proceeded a few hundred yards when a group of freedom fighters blocking the road fired at the car. I jumped out exclaiming 'Indian army'.

Seeing my olive green Indian Army uniform they stopped firing but wanted to kill the Pakistani chief of staff. I reasoned with them, trying to persuade them to allow us to proceed. They reluctantly agreed. Meanwhile the press caught up with us. The *Time Magazine* correspondent reported that I had threatened to 'shoot you fellows'. I was unarmed! After a few minutes we were allowed to proceed. I entered Niazi's office. Present there were the seniormost Pakistani army, navy, and air force officers, as also some other senior military officers. I was shocked to see Maj. Gen. Nagra seated on the sofa with his arm around Niazi engaged in cracking bawdy jokes in Punjabi. Siddiq Salik in his book *Witness to Surrender* (1977) wrote that the jokes were unprintable!

We had moved Nagra just a few days earlier to replace Maj. Gen. Gurbax Singh, who was in command of the force that was moving to capture Dacca, but was wounded. Nagra had known Niazi from before when he was posted as military advisor to our High Commission in Islamabad. The ceasefire had taken effect at 1700 hours on 15 December. On the morning of 16 December, Nagra, who was some 30 miles outside Dacca with elements of 95 Mountain Brigade and 2 Para, well after the ceasefire went into force, sent a message to Niazi to send his representative. Niazi was at a loss to understand this message as he was expecting me. Nagra, flying a white flag, was escorted to Niazi's headquarters. I saw the three jeeps with white flags parked outside.

I called Nagra outside, gave him a sharp dressing down for disgraceful conduct unbecoming of a general officer. I told him to send some troops into Dacca, to the airfield and Intercontinental Hotel to protect the officials there. I also instructed him to arrange a table and two chairs at the Race Course for signature of The Instrument of Surrender, as also to provide a detachment for a joint guard of honour. I told him to leave behind a jeep for me. Nagra's later conduct was questionable. He hijacked Maj. Gen. Rao Farman Ali's new Mercedes and drove off with it to his former HQ in Assam. He was ordered to hand it over to command HQ, where it was taken on charge and given a registration number by Army HQ. There were several other allegations against the general. Aurora declined to recommend him for any decoration and wanted to institute disciplinary proceedings against him. He however reconsidered the matter and decided not to.

I re-entered the building. The draft Instrument of Surrender was read out. Niazi, with tears rolling down his cheeks, said: 'Who said I am surrendering? You have only come to discuss a ceasefire and withdrawal as proposed by me.' The service chiefs present also voiced their objections. Rao Farman Ali objected to surrendering to a 'Joint Command'. Time was running out so I called Niazi aside. I told him that if he did not surrender I could not take responsibility for the safety of their families and ethnic minorities but if he did I would ensure their protection. I asked him to reconsider, again reminding him that if he did not surrender I would not be responsible for the safety of their families. I then added that I would give him 30 minutes to reconsider and if he did not I would order the resumption of hostilities and the bombing of Dacca. I then walked out to be met by the press. I was extremely worried. Niazi had 26,400 troops in Dacca, we had about 3,000 some 30 miles out. I was in a quandary as what to do in the event of his refusing. Aurora and his entourage were expected to land in an hour or two and the ceasefire was to expire shortly. I had nothing in hand. The Pakistan Commission of Enquiry report later stated 'there was Gen. Jacob pacing outside, calmly puffing his pipe'. Far from it, I was extremely worried and tense. I spoke to the Pakistani sentry asking him about his family. He burst into tears saying that I as an Indian officer was talking to him whilst his own officers did not. After 30 minutes I walked into the office to be met by a deathly silence, my draft surrender document lying on the table. I asked Niazi if he accepted this document, to which he did not reply. I repeated the enquiry thrice. He still did not respond. I then picked up the document, holding it high, and said 'I take it as accepted'. Tears rolled down Niazi's cheeks, there were glares from those present. I called Niazi aside and then told him that I had arranged for the signing to take place at the Race Course in public. He objected strongly. I then told him that he would have to surrender his sword. He said that he did not have a sword but would surrender his revolver. I then told him he would have to provide a guard of honour. My thoughts went back to 1945 just after the Japanese surrender. When I landed in Sumatra, the Japanese provided me with a guard of honour. Niazi said there was no one to command it. I pointed to his ADC and said that he should command it. I permitted them to retain their weapons for their protection until such time as we could disarm them.

I then discussed with his chief of staff other modalities regarding the surrender of other garrisons and troops. I tried to get through on the wireless to Aurora who could not be contacted. Apparently he had gone to Agartala to pick up Gen. Sagat Singh. We then moved to the Mess for lunch. Gavin Young of the *Observer* was standing outside and requested if he could have lunch. We moved to the dining room. I was taken aback to see the tables properly set and loaded with silver trophies. I did not feel like eating and moved to one side. Gavin Young did a two-page piece for his paper the *Observer*, 'The Surrender Lunch'. At around 1560 hours, I asked Niazi to accompany me to the airport. As Nagra had not left a jeep for me, I sat with Niazi in his staff car. The Mukti Bahini fighters jumped on the car and it was with some difficulty that we reached the airport. Fortunately, en route we stopped a jeep with two of our paratroopers who were sightseeing. I asked them to follow us.

Nagra had not sent any troops to the airfield. I sent my staff officer to go and see if he could get some troops, some of whom should be entering the city. A little while later a truck loaded with armed Mukti Bahini arrived at the airfield. A man wearing our olive green uniform, wearing the badges of rank of a major general approached us, followed by two armed men. I placed him as 'Tiger' Siddiqui and sensed trouble. Siddiqui, who had some 20,000 fighters, did not fire a shot to halt the Pakistanis retreating through Tangail and did not move with us to Dacca. I felt that he had come to kill Niazi. I had to ensure that Niazi lived to sign the Instrument of Surrender. I told the two paratroopers to cover Niazi and point their rifles at Siddiqui.

I politely asked Siddiqui to leave the airfield. He did not respond. I repeated this request. He still did not respond. I then shouted to him to get his truckload of fighters off the airfield, and heaved a sigh of relief when they left. A few days later Siddiqui called the international media with their camera crews to witness the public bayoneting of people he called traitors. These pictures were later widely circulated.

Around 1630 hours Aurora and his entourage arrived in a fleet of five M14 and four Allouette helicopters. Aurora was accompanied by his wife and the navy and air force chiefs. Lt Gen. Sagat Singh and some of his divisional commanders also alighted, as did Wing Commander Khondker. Osmani, unfortunately was not there; the helicopter in which he had been travelling having been shot at and damaged. I had planned to travel in the last car with Aurora and Niazi, but Aurora asked me to make way for his wife, who then took her place by her husband's side. The ADC, who was carrying the papers to be signed and I had to hitch our way on a truck to the Race Course. Though there was very little time for any preparations, the ceremony went off reasonably well. After inspecting the guard of honour, Aurora and Niazi sat at the table and signed the Instrument of Surrender. I glanced at the documents and was aghast to see the heading which read 'Instrument of Surrender – to be signed at 1631 IST [Indian Standard Time]'. I looked at my watch, which showed that the time was 1655 hours. The documents they brought to be signed had to be re-signed by both in Calcutta some two weeks later!

Niazi removed his epaulette, took out his revolver and handed it to Aurora; tears rolled down his cheeks. It was getting dark. The crowd at the Race Course began shouting and there were threats to lynch Niazi; anti-Pakistani slogans and abuses resounded. They then moved towards Niazi. The senior officers present formed a cordon around him and whisked him off in one of our jeeps.

I briefed Lt Gen. Sagat Singh regarding the disarming of the Pakistanis and other modalities. We then returned to the airfield. Rear Admiral Shariff, whom I had given permission to meet our naval commander, met Vice Admiral Krishnan. Krishnan asked Shariff to hand over his pistol to him, which he did. We then took off for Agarthala and thence to Calcutta.

I wondered why 1631 hours (4.31 p.m.) was the time specified for signature of the Instrument of Surrender. Parliament was in session so perhaps Manekshaw had told Indira Gandhi that it would be signed at that time. Members were anxious to know what was happening. According to Siddhartha Shankar Ray, the chief minister of West Bengal, who was present in parliament that day, members were anxious to know about the progress of negotiations. The minister of defence repeatedly stated that Gen. Jacob was having lunch. It was most ironic that amidst all these tumultuous events, Jacob would be remembered by posterity for enjoying a very long and leisurely lunch!

Sometime later, when I examined the revolver that Niazi had surrendered, I realized that it could not have been Niazi's. The barrel was choked with muck and had not been cleaned for some considerable time, the lanyard was frayed and dirty. This could not have been the personal weapon of a commanding general. Niazi had probably taken it from one of the military policemen and surrendered it as his personal weapon. I could not help feeling that in a small way Niazi had got some of his own back.

The military operations have been described as a 'lightning campaign' and is studied in military institutions in many countries. In the words of a later Pakistani document of the war with the National Defence College of Pakistan:

> The Indians planned and executed their offensive against East Pakistan in a textbook manner. It was a classic example of thorough planning, minute coordination, and bold execution. The credit clearly goes to General Jacob's meticulous preparations in the Indian Eastern Command and its implementation by his corps commanders.

Niazi had proposed a ceasefire under UN auspices, withdrawal under the UN, hand over of the government to the UN, and no reprisals. There was no mention of India in his ceasefire proposal. On 16 December he had 26,400 troops in Dacca, we some 3000 outside. The UN Security Council was in session debating a Polish Resolution. He could have fought on for at least two more weeks, and had he fought on for even one more day, the UN Security Council would have ordered a withdrawal. Some Pakistanis say that Niazi's nerve broke and that I bluffed him into surrendering. I negotiated the surrender on my unconfirmed draft document that I had sent to Delhi. It would perhaps be pertinent to quote the Pakistan Government's Hamood-ur-Rehman Commission of Enquiry Report:

> General Niazi, when you had 26,400 troops in Dacca and the Indians a few thousand outside you could have fought on for at least two more weeks, with the UN Security Council in session. Had you fought on for even one more day the Indians would have had to go back, why then did you accept a shameful unconditional public surrender and provide a guard of honour commanded by your ADC?
>
> Niazi: I was compelled to do so by Jacob who blackmailed me into surrendering …

This he has repeated in his book *The Betrayal of East Pakistan*, published in 1988.

Suppose I had failed in Dacca to convert the ceasefire under the UN as proposed by Niazi into an unconditional public surrender, the only one in history, we would have had to go back the next day. I did not fail and India became a regional superpower. The campaign was indeed a 'very close run thing'. We were extremely lucky. The campaign, though studied by armies abroad, is not studied in much detail in India, nor have the lessons from it, particularly mobility and logistics, been given sufficient weightage.

A ceasefire was converted into a surrender and signed in the space of some four hours. The modalities for the ceremony were basic and were arranged with meagre resources. To quote the Duke of Wellington again after Waterloo: 'It was a close run thing!'

The Pakistanis have no love for the Jews. The Pakistanis are well aware that I am a Jew. It is therefore surprising that in their study at the Pakistan National Defence College on the 1971 war in East Pakistan, they give credit for the Indian victory clearly to 'Maj. Gen. Jacob'. In India, however, my contribution to the 'textbook' campaign and in converting a ceasefire into an unconditional public surrender, the only one in history, is not widely known. I would like to reiterate that when my book *Surrender at Dacca: Birth of a Nation* was published in 1997. I personally gave Manekshaw and Aurora copies of it at a time when they were both fit and active; neither issued any rejoinder. The book has been translated into Chinese, Thai, Persian, Arabic, Bengali, and Hebrew.

The members of the team deputed to write the history of the 1971 war came to see me regarding the 1971 war. They had earlier met Manekshaw, Aurora, Sagat Singh, and Inder Gill. They had not planned to meet me until Gill told them that the only one who could give them an authoritative account of events was Jacob. I briefed them. They looked puzzled as they had been given highly coloured accounts from those interviewed earlier. Brig. Bhimayya, who was assisting the team, got them to see the operation instructions, and all the signals issued, including those ordering the brigades back to the Chinese border and the one of 13 December from Manekshaw, copied to the corp commanders ordering us to return to capture the towns we had bypassed and making no mention of Dacca. Bhimayya told me later that the Ministry of Defence decided that Mankeshaw's and not my account should be accepted.

Raising the XVI Corps

After the war was over, Manekshaw was very nice to me. I was promoted to raise a new XVI Corps south of the Pir Panjal Range of mountains. Before assuming command I spent a few days in Kashmir fishing my favourite trout beats. I was lucky to land my quota of six fish at Kokernag, all over four pounds. The photo of the catch was used by the Kashmir Tourism Department in their tourist brochure.

Aurora approached Mrs Indira Gandhi, seeking to be appointed a governor. She declined. He then approached the Akali government in the Punjab, and they later arranged a seat for him in the Rajya Sabha.

Lt Gen. P.S. Bhagat, VC, was appointed army commander in the newly constituted Northern Command which was my XVI Corp's immediate superior. HQ XVI Corps's responsibility stretched from the Pir Panjal Range to just across the Ravi river. I had to find a suitable site for the corps headquarters, and Jammu was suggested. This I promptly rejected as I did not wish the headquarters to be boxed up in that city. I remembered Nagrota from my days in Samba where I fished for mahseer in the river Tawi that flowed nearby. There was a tiny forest resthouse perched on a cliff overlooking the river from where the view was spectacular. I had it rented as my residence. There was hardly any infrastructure in Nagrota; we concentrated our energies on providing electricity and water.

Raising a corps headquarters is an onerous business. We were soon to be involved in numerous clashes with Pakistani troops on the border. The army commander, Lt. Gen. Bhagat was pragmatic and capable, and gave me a free hand. . He was fond of mixing with people and loved attending parties. As the only serving Victoria Cross awardee, he was the envy of the top brass in Delhi.

There were several incursions by Pakistani troops along the line of control, some quite major, involving many actions to evict them. Bhagat was assigned the task of delimiting the line of control consequent to the changes to the old ceasefire line up to the ceasefire of 17 December 1971. Bhagat chose to use the old 1 inch (1:63,360) to 1 mile map rather than the new 1:50,000 maps. The Pakistanis were using their new over 1:50,000 maps. It was problematic aligning the line of control on maps of different scales. Bhagat inadvertently made a mistake regarding Thakur Chak. While the line of control was to be drawn in relation to the positions held up to the ceasefire, the international border between Jammu and Pakistan could not be changed. Thakur Chak held by Pakistan was on our side of the international border but Bhagat erroneously treated it as part of the line of control and handed it over to Pakistan. I objected strongly but the matter took some time to be resolved in our favour.

I had a very high observation tower built at Thakur Chak which permitted observation of Sialkot and deep into Pakistan. I had a road built linking the various pickets, and this was defiladed from observation and provided for rapid movement along the picket line. I was able to spend some time fishing for mahseer. A little upstream from the resthouse I caught a 40 pound mahseer on very light tackle, which took me all of 40 minutes to land!

Gen Bhagat had perforce to retire because the then chief of army staff, Gen. G.G. Bewoor, was given an extension. If this had not been given, Bhagat would have normally become the next army chief, a position he had set his heart on occupying. Sadly this was not to be. He spent his last day of service with me. He was given the assignment of heading the Damodar Valley Corporation, with his office in Calcutta. Bhagat left my residence with tears in his eyes. Later in Calcutta, he fell seriously ill and died holding my hand muttering 'I want to go on a gun carriage'. We organized a fitting farewell for him. Gen. J.N. Chaudhari, former army chief, travelled with me, following the cortège. He turned round to me and said, 'Jacob, I hope I get a funeral as good as this'.

L.K. Jha was the governor of Jammu & Kashmir, and during the winter months he was based quite close to our headquarters and visited me frequently. Later, in Delhi when he was living at 10 Janpath, he invited me frequently to dine and chat. L.K. Jha was highly intelligent and close to Indira Gandhi. She used him as a channel to clarify certain problems. I lost a friend when he passed away.

On one of my trips to Delhi, I went to see Manekshaw who was staying in the MES Inspection Bungalow. He was sitting alone on the lawn and seemed depressed. He told me that he had requested Mrs Gandhi to appoint him deputy chairman of the Planning Commission, and that she had declined, offering him the post of High Commissioner to Canada instead. I felt sorry for him. My posting orders to Eastern Command as the army commander (GOC-in-C) arrived and I prepared to move to Calcutta.

11

My Days as Army Commander

I took over as GOC-in-C Eastern Command on 1 August 1974. I was back in the city of Calcutta where I was born; a city of friendly people and a city I loved. I moved into Army House in Alipore, a large unpretentious bungalow with a common wall abutting Calcutta Zoo. The building was acquired for Gen. Kumaramanglam when he took over as army commander. Kumaramanglam refused to move in, preferring to stay at Watergate House in Fort William. Sam Manekshaw was its first occupant. Incidentally, had I been given the choice I would have preferred to have gone back to Watergate House which I had occupied as chief of staff, Eastern Command.

Soon after I assumed command, the inspector general of police of Mizoram was shot dead in his office by a Mizo insurgent, Kapuchunga. I rushed to Aizwal, reviewed the situation, and ordered a revamping of operations. Meanwhile, in Nagaland the situation was deteriorating. There was an ambush near divisional headquarters and the GOC's 8 Mountain Division's helicopter was hit by small-arms fire. My predecessor had informed the army chief that he had broken the back of the Naga revolt and the two brigades could be withdrawn. These were de-inducted before he left. I assessed the situation. Troops were committed to static posts, leaving no reserves. I requested the army chief for more troops, but he quoted my predecessor's comment that the Naga insurgency had been crushed. I then reorganized the deployment at the various static posts, creating a reserve force of three battalions for mobile operations. I was approached by someone who claimed to be from RAW to use Agent Orange some 50 yards on either side of the main roads. I rejected the idea outright!

During October 1974, our troops partially intercepted a Naga gang on their way to China to collect arms and ammunition. The leading platoon of a Kumaon battalion had Muivah in their sights. They did not fire, awaiting reinforcements. Muivah got away leaving behind his diary. He is still very active and is currently located with his insurgents in Burma. I was amazed to read in his diary about his views on communism. Other documents captured revealed their detailed and thorough system of accounting. Soon after, Joshi of the Intelligence Bureau phoned me that he had class one information that a large gang was assembling to go to China. I asked him if he was sure as I intended to move a large number of troops from within and without Nagaland to intercept this gang. He replied that he was positive and gave me their last known location but was unable to predict their route across Nagaland. I thanked him. For the inner and outer cordons we needed some 8000 troops. I had to recourse to what we did for operations in East Pakistan in 1971, i.e. moving troops from the Chinese border. I ordered an infantry brigade to move directly into the outer cordon. The inner cordon was to be formed by the troops we had made mobile from units in Nagaland. The GOC of the division was on leave so the governor, L.P. Singh, phoned me to recall him. I informed the governor that there was no need to recall him, as I intended to personally oversee the operation. I spoke to the chief minister Vizol Angami and requested him to go to the neighbouring villages near where we expected the gang to move and to ask the villagers not to help them. Vizol was formerly in the underground. Vizol replied, 'What you are asking me to do is to commit political suicide'. I replied that he had earlier told me that the Chinese communists were a godless people so why was he doing nothing to stop them from going to China to collect weapons and to be brainwashed by the Chinese with godless communist propaganda. Vizol stared at me for a few minutes and then replied, 'General I will go; give me a helicopter to take me to these villages'. A helicopter was provided to him, and he as promised visited these villages, and his visits did make an impact. We were able to catch up with the gang near Mokochaung. We cordoned off the area, and while I was camping in the vicinity, the governor phoned asking me to allow Vamuzo, a minister with current links to the underground to negotiate with the gang. I felt that Vamuzo's aim was to gain time and let the gang slip away and told the governor so. The governor then asked me if I had imposed 'martial law'. I replied that he knew very well that we were operating under the Armed Forces Special Powers Act, and as such I declined to let Vamuzo go to negotiate. When the cordon closed in they did not find the gang. The brigade commander, Brig. Kler felt that the gang had got away and recommended that the troops move to the next stop line in Tuensang. I reluctantly agreed, and took a chopper to the Assam Rifles post at Chintungia in the general area where the gang was supposed to be. I spoke to the Gorkha post commander and sought to know how the gang could have broken through. He shook his head, 'Sahib they are still there'. I asked him how he knew. He again replied, 'Sahib I don't know, but I do know that they are still there'. The troops were about to move to their next stop line so I had to make a quick decision. My ADC, Capt. Harbux Singh Gill, handed me some pineapple which the post commander had given him. It was the sweetest pineapple I had ever tasted. I thought for a few minutes and got on the radio to the brigade commander and ordered him to about face and go in again. I told him to fire 3 inch mortar smoke into the area (non-phosphorus). The operation was a success. Apart from one or two, the entire gang was captured. It was indeed a lucky stroke of fate. Mrs Rano Shaiza (Naga leader Phizo's niece) accused me of using poison gas but subsequently recanted and wrote to thank me for what I had done for the Naga people. (*See* Appendix.)

During an insurgency there are two factors necessary to keep it from developing firm bases and lines of supply of arms and ammunition. We had broken their supply line to China, and then went for their bases in Nagaland. The insurgents were on the run and sent feelers for peace. Meetings were held in Chedema and eventually they agreed to sign the Shillong Accord. The governor asked me or my representative to go to Shillong to sign the Accord but I declined because Clause 3 could provide loopholes in the future for the insurgents to rescind from it (*see* 'Excerpts from Letters, Rano Shaiza and Governor' in appendix).

The Mizo insurgency was in full swing. The Mizo Hills were originally called the Lushai Hills, *lushai* meaning long head. We were fortunate in having Ajit Doval, a young Intelligence Bureau (IB) officer. Doval was a livewire and had guts, venturing in disguise into territory controlled by the hostiles. We had some professional differences. I recall one such: the pursuit of Biakvella's gang which was moving from Manipur to Mizoram. I wanted to apprehend them, Doval to negotiate. He did not inform us that he was moving some of them in an IB jeep and I ordered the jeep to be intercepted and the hostiles to be apprehended. There was a hue and cry from Delhi. The army chief, Gen. T.N. 'Tappy' Raina, phoned me to hand them back to the IB. I told him that according to the law, I could interrogate the hostiles for 14 days, after which they were to be handed over to the nearest police station. Raina said I was being difficult, and I told him (he was in my platoon in the Officers Training School and was commissioned some months before me because I was sent for further training to the Artillery School) that he had no 'locus standi' in the matter and that we would hand them over to the nearest police station in accordance with the law and not to the IB. Doval performed excellently in arranging for the hostile leaders to attend a conference in Calcutta. There were protracted negotiations leading to a peace agreement that still stands. Doval was indeed the most outstanding IB officer I had the good fortune to work with. During this period I also dealt with Ramji Kao, who set up the RAW. Kao too was an outstanding officer and a thinker. Later I had arranged to have the Lushai song 'Lendupui' set to music by Joseph as a march, 'Hanste Lushai' (The laugh of the Lushai).

I had known Palden Thendup Namgyal, who became the 12th Chogyal of Sikkim, since 1969. From the earliest times the population of Sikkim was predominantly Lepcha–Bhutia. There were subsequently large influxes of Nepalese, altering ethnic balances. On 5 December 1950, after long negotiations, Sikkim became an Indian protectorate. The Chogyal's first wife Sangey Dei died in June 1957. They had a son Wangchuk. The Chogyal then married an American named Hope Cooke in March 1963. They had two sons Tensing and Palden. Palden Namgyal was crowned Chogyal, after his father's death on 4 April 1965.

Meanwhile, there was much political ferment, some allege instigated by Delhi. Eventually, in 1953, a parity formula for seat sharing in the State Council between the Lepcha–Bhutia combine and the Nepalese was worked out. There was much opposition in Delhi to Hope Cooke. When she left the Chogyal and returned to America, the government of India heaved a sigh of relief. I found the Chogyal a pleasant man, a touch pompous but someone who, if handled properly, would have cooperated. However, the political officers in Gangtok disliked him and worked for his removal. In March 1975, Lt Gen. Jaswant Singh from Army HQ arrived at my office in Fort William on the orders of Kewal Singh, the foreign secretary. He told me that Kewal Singh had instructed him to have the Sikkim Guard disarmed and disbanded as they feared they would help the Chogyal to cross over to China! This was preposterous. Incidentally, earlier when the Chogyal had come to visit me at Command House, Alipore, his car was followed into the building by a truck-load of policemen. I called the assistant commissioner of police in charge and asked him what the problem was. He replied that the police were there to prevent the Chogyal going to China. I told him not to be silly as there was no way the Chogyal could go to China from here and that he should immediately remove his police from my residence. I told Lt Gen. Jaswant Singh that he could go to Gangtok but I would not permit anyone there to deal with him. I then asked him if the army chief knew about this. He said he did not know. I then phoned General Bewoor. Bewoor said he knew nothing about this and that Kewal Singh, the foreign secretary, who was camping at Gangtok should speak to him. The message was passed to Kewal Singh, who said he had no desire to speak to Bewoor. I had a message passed to Kewal Singh that I had issued instructions to the corps and division headquarters that no officer would take orders from him. I sent my brigadier general, staff, Brig. Baljit Mehta to Gangtok, with the brief that only orders from command HQ sent through him would be acted on. I tried to impress on Bewoor that he should convey to the government that a Lepcha Chogyal, even if arrogant, could be handled. Soon after, Bewoor phoned me that the government had decided that the Sikkim Guard would be disarmed as they were a security threat. I said that I knew the Sikkim Guard and they did not constitute any threat whatsoever. He said these were the orders of the government. I asked for this to be given in writing. He said that there would be nothing in writing, only verbal orders. I was most unhappy about the whole affair. I spoke to Brig. Baljit Singh to work out with the Division HQ the modalities to disarm the Guard, stressing that the operation should be bloodless. Unfortunately, one of the sentries of the palace guard fired at our troops and was shot dead. The armoury was seized and the guard disarmed and later disbanded. The Chogyal was in tears. He dipped a cloth into the blood of a soldier and requested time and time again for the colours and standard of the Guard to be given to him. This was refused by the government. The entire incident was unnecessary and deplorable. It was given out again and again that the Chogyal would use the guard to escort him to China! (The guard, armed only with rifles, was just 200 strong!). Later the Chogyal's son Tensing had a shout out with his father and thrashed him, whereupon the Chogyal in despair took an overdose of sleeping pills. I was informed of this and immediately ordered an army helicopter to fly him to the airport to be airlifted to Calcutta. He was admitted to a private hospital where, after a few days, he recovered consciousness. I met Tensing outside his room in the hospital, unrepentant. The Chogyal died in 1982 and Tensing was killed in a car accident on 11 March 1978. Some have alleged that the latter was not an accident.

Capt W.A. Sangma was chief minister of Meghalaya, heading the APHLC, a regional political party in the early 1970s. He was a competent chief minister and led a clean government. We had a very good working relationship and met frequently in Shillong. He, after some time, came to see me in Calcutta. He had taken over as chief minister on 18 March 1972. One evening in 1976 he called me in Calcutta asking for my advice. He said that the Congress party wanted his party to join them. I asked him whether he wanted to, to which he replied in the negative. I said that he should do whatever he considered to be right.

Two weeks later he joined the Congress. When I met him later I asked him what had made him change his mind. He replied that it had been conveyed to him that if he did not join the Congress there would be very serious consequences. Later, during one of my meetings with Indira Gandhi at Raj Bhawan, Shillong, the subject turned to the regional governments in the NE. Indira Gandhi said that these regional governments should all join the Congress. I mentioned that in these areas of insurgency it would be more expedient to have a nationalist regional government through which the central government could deal with these insurgents rather than dealing with them directly. Mrs Gandhi was firm in her view that regional governments should join the Congress, as had the Sangma government. I said: 'Madam Prime Minister, I get more cooperation from these regional governments than any of the Congress governments.' It was a tactless remark and Mrs Gandhi was furious. After a while she calmed down and said, 'Go on'. I replied that I wondered whether she would like me to tell her what she would like to hear, rather what the realities were. She did not respond. Mrs Gandhi enjoyed having a break in Raj Bhawan, Shillong. I had to brief her several times there and have the highest regard for her. She had great courage and dignity. She sometimes relaxed and spoke about her children, Rajiv and Sanjay. She mentioned that Sanjay did not eat between meals, but that Rajiv snacked often in between them. She confided to me that her favourite musical was *Fiddler on the Roof*, and once asked me why the Jews were leaving India. I did not answer.

Here I must mention one particular exchange regarding the Golden Temple. I strongly advised against any forcible entry into the Golden Temple, mentioning to L.K. Jha that in 1922-3 there were some problems the British had with a gurdwara a few miles north of Amritsar. They put a barbed wire fence around it and controlled entry to the temple but did not enter the temple. This was duly conveyed to Mrs Gandhi by Jha. Most unfortunately the Golden Temple was forcibly entered with heavy loss of life.

After this event Mrs Gandhi sent for me but the message was not conveyed to me by Narasimha Rao who was dealing with Punjab on behalf of the party. Narasimha Rao sent for me and asked me to tour Punjab and give him a brief for Mrs Gandhi. I spent seven days touring Punjab, having discussions with all sections of the people there, and gave the report to Rao. Discussions of my recommendations were spread over two days, and that is the last I heard of the matter.

In my opinion, in the matter of imposing the Emergency, Mrs Indira Gandhi was badly advised by S.S. Ray, the chief minister of West Bengal. Ray boasted that he was close to Mrs Gandhi and that not only had he advised her on its imposition but had drafted the ordinance.

One of my concerns during my tenure as GOC-in-C Eastern Command was the large-scale infiltration of Bangladeshis into Assam and Tripura. On a visit to Agartala, the chief secretary informed me that the chief minister of Tripura, Sen Gupta, was openly encouraging the entry of Bangladeshis into Tripura in order to change the ethnic balances in order to counter tribal votes. I went to see the chief minister and apprised him of this infiltration. He said that he had the 'blessings of Mrs Gandhi for this'. I checked with the army chief who reverted after a few hours that no such approval had been given. I then went to see the chief minister with the chief secretary. He asked the chief secretary to leave, but I told the chief minister that it was important that he be present. I then went on to tell the chief minister that I had checked with Delhi and that no approval had been given for the induction of Bangladeshis into Tripura. He scowled: 'How does this affect you?' I replied that this infiltration was a threat to national security and as I was responsible to the government for national security, this unauthorized induction would have to stop. I would ask the Border Security Force to take the necessary steps to stop this illegal immigration. We then left his office.

In another serious case in West Bengal, I was asked to meet R. Parthasarathy, foreign policy adviser to the prime minister and the foreign secretary, Jagat Mehta. Jagat Mehta informed me that 'Tiger Siddiqui' of the 1971 war notoriety, who had publicly bayoneted people he called traitors a few days after the surrender, was in West Bengal with an armed group of his followers. Siddiqui was thoroughly untrustworthy and I was at a loss to understand what he was doing here. I told Jagat to tell Parthasarathy that I could not for reasons of national security accept this. Jagat replied that Parthasarathy would not listen to him and that I should tell him. I went up to Parthasarathy and told him that this was unacceptable.

He looked at me and pouted his lips, not responding. I said that as I was responsible for the security in the region I could not accept having an armed group of foreigners on Indian soil. He just stared at me. I then said that I would evict them. Siddiqui and his armed gang of followers moved back to Bangladesh shortly after.

When I took over command, a Congress government was in place in Writers' Building, headed by Siddartha Shankar Ray with whom I was on first-name terms. Ray was a thorough gentleman, something of a social snob who frequently referred to his elite family background. He did not drink or smoke, and was very fond of sports, particularly cricket. A day before the 'Emergency' was declared he called me over the phone and said, 'Jake I have some very confidential information for your ears only; there is going to be an emergency'. I was at a loss to understand what he was talking about. I retorted, 'Siddharth, what emergency; I was driving around Calcutta, everything was normal.' He responded, 'You will see tomorrow. There will be a national emergency throughout the country.' The Emergency was declared the next day and Ray had a major role in advising it and in drafting the emergency orders.

Ray thought he could ride roughshod over everyone. He came to official functions well past the designated time and deliberately after the arrival of the governor, John Dias, a former ICS officer. When I asked Ray why he behaved in this way, he replied 'I treat him as my doormat'.

Ray decided to build a pavilion in the Eden Gardens Cricket stadium without clearance from the army. Eden Gardens is part of the 'Maidan' and under the army's control. It is governed by the Fort William Act, promulgated by the British to ensure that the fields of fire from the Fort William cannon of an earlier day were unhampered. Magisterial powers were vested with the garrison commander. On seeing the report in the newspapers I summoned the commissioner of police, rebuked him, and ordered him to issue a warrant stopping work on the pavilion. A few days later Ray telephoned me asking me to discuss some matters in his office in Writers' Buildings. I entered his office and he asked me to be seated. He passed the warrant on to me. I looked at it and said that it had been issued under my orders. He said, 'But Jake I am the chief minister.' I retorted, 'You have no more right to build on the Maidan than I have to build a penthouse on top of your "Writers' buildings".' He replied, 'But the pavilion is necessary.' I said, 'I agree and would have sanctioned it had you asked for sanction, but you did not.' He replied, 'I will speak to Bansi Lal, the defence minister.' He picked up the phone and spoke to the minister. He then put down the phone, smiled, and said, 'Bansi Lal says that if you agree he will agree.' I said the question of Bansi Lal agreeing did not arise as powers are only entrusted to the garrison commander under the Fort William Act. He then came back, 'I am looking for someone like you to run Calcutta and its environs. When are you retiring?' This upset me even more. I replied, 'Chief minister, I do not require a job from you when I retire,' and took my leave.

The chief minister approached Indira Gandhi. Gen. Raina, the army chief phoned asking me to grant permission. I told him that he had no locus standi in this matter and I would do what had to be done. Several other approaches were made. After two months, the chief minister asked me to attend a meeting with him and the minister concerned. The meeting was cordial. I had come prepared with my proposals for a resolution of the matter. I said we would permit construction subject to:

(a) As the state government had encroached on 1.5 acres of land on the Maidan, it would have to hand over 78 acres of land in the Salt Lake area. This figure was based on the then value of land in the respective areas.
(b) A specific number of seats would be reserved for the army in the pavilion and stadiums.
(c) The concrete stand, illegally built on the Mohan Bagan ground, would be used by spectators from the army.
(d) The other minor encroachments would be removed.
(e) A percentage of the gate money from grounds on the Maidan would be spent on army welfare.

The chief minister retorted, 'Jake I did not realize you were a real estate agent.' I ignored the remark and said, 'This is a final offer, take it or leave it.' Ray's prestige was at stake in relation to the construction of the pavilion. He looked at me and said, 'Jake you are a tough man.' I immediately sent a survey party to fence in the 78 acres. (Today the West Bengal government is requesting the army to swap the land with alternative land in Behala). By the time I left, the state government implemented all the stipulated conditions, except that relating to gate money. Siddharth, when alive, and his charming wife, Maya, were amongst my small circle of close friends. I have the highest regard for both. I called on them on 17 December 2010 at their residence in Calcutta. Regrettably Ray passed away recently.

The Congress ministry was replaced by a Marxist one headed by Jyoti Basu. I got on well with Jyoti Basu and his government. They were pragmatic and easy to work with and made no demands. Jyoti Basu was a pragmatic statesman.

Bansi Lal was the defence minister and with him I established an excellent rapport. He required an hour's briefing on every visit of his to Calcutta. Briefings took place in the operations room at Fort William. I took him around the command for him to get a feel of the problems our troops were facing. We toured Mizoram, Tripura, Manipur, Nagaland, Assam, Arunachal, and Sikkim. When visiting the Se La defences we ran into the memorial tablet of the late Brig. Hoshiar Singh, who was killed during the operations. Bansi Lal turned round to me, 'General Sahib, don't you agree that Jats are the world's best soldiers'. I paused, and then replied that anyone with good training and motivation could make a good soldier. He was still looking at me for an answer. I then said that if he asked me which units excelled in the operations in East Pakistan I could tell him. He said, 'Which units?' I replied, 'The Bihar Regiment'. He gave a grunt. We walked down the line of soldiers. He asked one of them where he was from. He replied that he was from Ranchi. Bansi Lal put his arm around my shoulder and said, 'General Sahib, from your home place'.

Bansi Lal was pragmatic and had a sound understanding of the geo–military environment. I explained to him why it was necessary to control the entry and exits from the straits of Malacca. In 1971, the American *Enterprise* carrier group had moved through the straits of Malacca, through the great channel between Sumatra and the Great Nicobar and into the Indian Ocean. Our navy from their base in Campbell Bay were wholly unaware of its move. I told him that to control the straits of Malacca it was essential to have an air base in the Indira Point area. He agreed and sent a group of secretaries to examine the proposal. Up to now there has been no progress! Apparently there are concerns regarding Indonesian and Malayan reactions to our setting up a base there.

Jagjivan Ram, on one of his visits to Calcutta, asked me why I was providing a vehicle to Manekshaw on his business visits to Calcutta, saying that he had not been authorized a vehicle as field marshal. I replied that I was not providing him a vehicle as field marshal, but was providing a vehicle to all former Eastern Command army commanders, and Manekshaw was a former army commander.

Prinsep Ghat, on the River Hoogly, was under demolition to make way for a bridge. James Prinsep, a most distinguished scholar, had been able to decipher the inscriptions on the Ashoka pillars, which had till then been an enigma. Two granite lions decorated the ghat, one sleeping and one awake. I requested Chief Minister Jyoti Basu that they be given to the army in Fort William. Jyoti Basu readily agreed. Today they grace the entrance to the HQ Eastern Command Officers' Mess.

The mess was sparsely furnished. I donated my family mahogany dining table with dining chairs to seat thirty-six, a rosewood table to seat twelve, four marble-top tables, a roll-top desk, six old Chinese scrolls, and some modern paintings. I had spent the most important years of my life in Fort William, both as chief of staff and as army commander and attempted in some small measure to give back to the command to which I owed so much.

To raise money for the welfare of troops I organized a tattoo in Eden Gardens, moving in troops, tanks, and guns. This caused great consternation as it was rumoured that I was planning to stage a coup to take over the country! The commissioner of police told me that he had counted five tanks. I jokingly responded: 'One each for the five point crossing.' The Tattoo was a sell-out, and enabled us to raise a very large sum of money which we distributed for the welfare of the troops.

Meetings with Foreign Military Delegations

In early 1977, I was informed that an Iranian military delegation comprising some twenty senior officers had requested to meet me and be briefed on mountain warfare and also on mobile operations.

The delegation was led by the chief of army staff of the Iranian army, Gen. Abbassi Gharabaghi who claimed to also have links with the Savak, their intelligence organization. He was after the Shah, the most powerful man in Iran and was accompanied by his young wife. I briefed them on mobile operations.

We arranged demonstrations and lectures on mountain warfare in Sikkim. They were charmed by the beautiful environment of Sikkim and the unique culture of the people. They spent a great deal of time shopping, surprisingly for Sikkim-made carpets!

The delegation was very keen to return to Calcutta where a they frequented the Golden Slipper night club and other places of entertainment. They spent a great deal of time shopping in the various boutiques, buying expensive jewellery, silks, and other accessories.

I was taken aback when the I was told by Army Chief Abbassi that he did not trust his own army or their loyalty to the Shah. I reported this to Army HQ in Delhi as also to some diplomats of friendly countries in Calcutta. After some two weeks, the delegation left Calcutta. Other than Eastern Command, the delegation did not visit any other command. Gen. Abbassi died in exile in Paris some years later. Some six months thereafter, in July 1977, I received a phone call from the army chief in Delhi that an Iraqi military delegation had arrived in Delhi and had asked to meet me. I enquired what they wanted to discuss. They indicated that they wanted to meet me personally and have a private discussion with me, declining to provide further details. A delegation headed by Maj. Gen. Najdat Kassim Maksoud and some ten senior officers arrived at Fort William on 9 July 1977. After an exchange of pleasantries, Gen. Maksoud said that he knew of the campaign I had conducted in East Pakistan and also of my record in the Second World War, particularly of the amphibious operations in which I had participated. He was quite aware that I had had a brief spell of operational service in Iraq during the Second World War in 1942. He was also aware that my forbears had come from Iraq some 200 years earlier and that I was Jewish.

To my surprise he rolled out a map of the Shatt al Arab and placed it on my table. He then said that his government was aware of my military expertise and had sought my advice on how to counter an expected Iranian amphibious operation on the Ismuthus of Al Faw. I thought for a few minutes after studying the map, and said that as far as I was aware the Iranians did not have the amphibious capability to make such a landing. He then insisted that they would make the necessary arrangements, and asked what defensive measures they should take. I gave them some parameters for defensive measures in such an unlikely contingency, and went on to tell them that if the Iranians were to launch an offensive there, they should enter through the marshes. They questioned this and wanted to know how. I replied, 'In small boats.' They were not convinced, and the Iraqi delegation returned to Iraq shortly after. Many years later in the latter stages of the Iraqi–Iranian war, the Iranians did operate from small boats in the marshes.

I retired from the army on 31 July 1978 on completion of my four-year tenure as army commander. I drove out through East Gate, bringing back memories of the summer of 1941 when I had cycled through the then Plassey Gate to be interviewed for a commission in the Indian Army. I felt sorry to leave: thirty-seven years of soldiering had come to an abrupt end.

12

Retirement: Goa and Punjab

I moved to my house in Kalimpong. Kalimpong is an incredibly lovely town. The garden was in full bloom, the *azalea* and *hibiscus* hedges a riot of colour. The avocado trees were fruiting as were the peach and pear. I lay on the grass beneath a bright blue sky watching the clouds pass by. It was heaven. I returned to Calcutta, a city I love, a city in which I grew up and where the people are warm, friendly, and cultured. In the spring of 1979, I took over as chairman of a company dealing in commodity trading. There were problems amongst the staff at our Delhi office so I moved there to sort matters out, and then stayed on there.

Delhi is quite different from Calcutta; a bureaucratic city where I had served earlier, both in the city proper and the cantonment, and was well-acquainted with it. I was not very happy in the world of business and did not derive any job satisfaction. Soon after arriving in Delhi I received a phone call from the foreign secretary, Jagat Mehta from Calcutta inviting me to come to Calcutta to meet the King of Bhutan.

I knew the king, as also his late father, and used to visit Bhutan frequently. I was given the freedom to fish wherever I wished. In a mountain stream at some 11,000 feet, I caught a nine pound trout, a record. The king asked to see it, so I sent it to him.

The late king, his father, used to ask me to spend an hour or two with the young prince on my visits to brief him on matters of international relations, governance, and other related matters. I made many friends in Bhutan. After a pleasant meeting with the king, Jagat Mehta told me that I was to be appointed ambassador to Bhutan. I told Jagat that much as I liked Bhutan, I did not wish to accept the appointment. He told me that it was my duty to go there. I told him that he was no one to tell me where my duty lay. I bade the king goodbye and left for Delhi. Three months later I was again approached by Jagdish Hiremath of the Ministry of External Affairs to go to Bhutan as ambassador and again expressed my regrets.

I found doing business very difficult, involving many pressures with which I was not comfortable. I decided to leave in 1989, handing over my portfolio to the staff for a very nominal price.

In 1991, I was approached by Professor Manohar Sondhi to join the BJP. I considered the offer for some time, and after some three months agreed to join to advise in the fields of defence and foreign affairs.

At that time the BJP was just beginning to develop its personality as a party, claiming to be a 'party with a difference'. That difference, I feel, with the passage of time began eroding.

I was impressed by the president, Khushabhau Thakre, a simple and upright man. When he was dying of cancer in a tiny cubicle in the outhouse quarters of 11 Ashoka Road, I visited him regularly. He died after a long battle with cancer. The possessions he left behind were four sets of kurta-pyjamas and two pairs of slippers. He was a man I admired and will never forget.

Atal Behari Vajpayee kept much to himself, relying largely on Brajesh Misra for whom he developed a great fondness when he was foreign minister. Brajesh, then in the United Nations, looked after him during his visits there. Vajpayee was well versed in politics, a wonderful orator, and a popular prime minister.

Vajpayee, unlike Thakre, liked the good things and comforts of life: good food, fine drinks and music. He had a successful spell as prime minister. Unfortunately he relied a great deal on Pramod Mahajan, who he affectionately called 'Munda', whose business dealings were alleged to be questionable.

L.K. Advani is a likeable person, cultured and soft spoken. He was projected by the party as a 'Man of iron'. I got on well with him and his family. He was not a very good judge of people and relied on some with dubious records. He was a capable home minister, and could have produced better results had he not become over-burdened with excessive responsibilities. His staff was not well versed in matters of national security and were unable to make a positive impact on the law and order situation in the country in general, or the Naxalites and insurgencies in Jammu & Kashmir and the North East. There is a compelling need to meet the challenges of terrorism and the insurgencies sponsored by Pakistan's ISI and others by revamping the security agencies drawing upon the experience gained by the Department of Homeland Security in the US.

Advani's visit to Pakistan in 2008 was to have serious consequences. His praise of Mohammed Ali Jinnah did not go down well in India. There were large-scale protests all over the country. On returning to India he resigned as party president. I spoke to him over the phone advising him not to withdraw his resignation. I reminded him of the pressure exerted by Nehru on Gen. Thimayya to withdraw his resignation and after he agreed to withdraw it, Nehru went on to tell parliament that 'The army chief is impetuous; one day he resigns and the next day he takes back his resignation'. I then quoted Marcus Aurelius: 'To do what you feel is right instead of humbly saying Amen to what the world tells you is right, is to have kept your soul alive.' Advani withdrew his resignation, expressed his regrets, and withdrew his Karachi statement.

Dr Murli Manohar Joshi is a man of integrity and principle but unfortunately he does not wield much influence in the party. I found him to be most reasonable and pragmatic. When, as administrator of Chandigarh, I requested him to make up the deficiency of 550 teachers in the Union Territory, he did so, overruling the opposition from the IAS 'babus' in his ministry.

Pramod Mahajan, who as I said was very close to Vajpayee, raised funds for the party. Though he came from a modest background he maintained a lavish lifestyle and established close links with several business houses. When I was governor of Goa he phoned me asking me to do something not 'kosher'. I told him to get lost and not phone me to do what was improper, and thereafter whenever we subsequently met he did not conceal his dislike for me. People have told me the he did all he could to scuttle the proposal of the VHP to have me elected president! Mahajan's promising political career was cut short when he was shot dead by his brother.

Arun Jaitley is one of the younger potential leaders of the BJP. He is highly intelligent, a good debater and speaker, and is a brilliant and successful lawyer. He does not however like to work in harness.

Experiences in Goa

I was appointed governor of Goa on 19 April 1998. Goa is a beautiful state with lovely beaches and the verdant forests of the western ghats. From childhood I grew to love the forests, running water, mountains and the fauna and flora of the western ghats which were redolent with memories of the great Himalaya. Unfortunately, the hills were being ripped apart by open cast mining, the deep scars they left in the hills an environmental catastrophe.

I moved into Raj Bhawan. The building, once a convent, was over 350 years old and nestled atop a promontory. Once however there was a plague in Panjim, and the Portuguese governor had the convent moved out, and then subsequently moved into the convent buildings. There is a lovely old church in the complex. When I arrived, the promontory was collapsing into the sea. We had to drill into the hillside to stabilize the hill, and also placed tetra-pods on the waterline to dissipate the force of the waves. The roof of the building also leaked and major repairs to the structure had to be undertaken.

The drive into the Raj Bhawan was a kilometre long. We had pepper vines and breadfruit trees planted all along the tree-lined drive. It was Capt. Bligh's act of giving scarce supplies of water to the breadfruit saplings in preference to the crew of HMS *Bounty* that was the principal cause of the mutiny on the *Bounty*. The Portuguese brought into Goa the breadfruit tree and the chilli, and it was from there that the Mexican chilli from Mexico spread throughout the subcontinent.

Goa has forty elected MLAs, all with ambitions to become ministers, many vying to become chief minister. Politics in Goa is thus much akin to musical chairs. MLAs frequently cross the floor, allegedly for financial benefits or a ministerial berth. Pratap Singh Rane had been appointed chief minister on 16 December 1994 when Dr Wilfred D'Souza, together with ten MLAs, broke away from the Rane government. On 29 July 1998, I summoned Rane and told him that as he had lost his majority he should resign. Rane retorted that the Speaker had not recognized the group that had defected. I told him that if he did not resign I would have no option but to dismiss him. He then requested me not to do so and that he would resign on his own the following morning. I had my doubts but my staff said that he would keep his word. Next morning, when he did not do so, I phoned him and he told me that he would not resign.

The house was in session and the financial appropriations bill had to be passed. I had to act quickly. I issued instructions to the Speaker that the financial appropriations bill should first be considered and after that there should be a vote of confidence in the house. The finance bill was duly passed, but when the proceedings for the vote of confidence were held there was bedlam in the house with blows being exchanged. I received an intimation from the chief minister that he had won by a voice vote. This was followed by a letter from the Speaker that there was a division and that the Rane government had secured a majority, the votes of the 10 MLAs of the D'Souza group not having been entertained by him. I had two versions of the proceedings, Rane's and the Speaker's.

It was apparent that Rane had lost his majority. I sent him a letter under Article 174 of the Constitution dismissing him and asked D'Souza to form a government, giving him seven days to prove his majority, which he did. Parliament was in session and there was an uproar from the Congress. No Congress government had been dismissed for over twenty years. I was accused of malafide and raping the Constitution, and was on my own with the BJP benches remaining silent. Rane went to court and a bench of the Bombay High Court was convened. Rane had employed a very brilliant and powerful battery of lawyers, Parsaram, Kapil Sibal, and Fali Nariman. I had one lawyer, Sanghi. I did not wish to appear in court, so I got my secretary to present an affidavit on my behalf, assisting my lawyer to prepare the case.

The Bench set aside Rane's 'Malafide' plea and passed the severest strictures on the conduct of the Speaker. Rane then approached the Supreme Court and the proceedings there fizzled out. Wilfred D'Souza, towards the end of November 1998, decided to go to London with his wife. Whilst he was there defections were engineered and he lost his majority. He returned and tried to regain control but failed. At 1 a.m. on 26 November, I was woken up and told that D'Souza was waiting to hand in his resignation, which I accepted. I then asked Luizinho Falerio, who claimed to have a majority, to form a ministry. By early February, Falerio had lost his majority and no party was able to form a government. I then held discussions with all party leaders who agreed to give me in writing, attested by all their MLAs, a request for imposition of President's Rule.

The government did not have a majority in the upper house and without the request of all the MLAs, it would have been difficult to impose President's Rule. President's Rule was imposed without debate on 9 February 1999 and revoked on 9 June 1999. In the elections that took place towards the end of President's Rule, the Goa Peoples Party headed by Francisco Sardinia, a breakaway group of the INC supported by the BJP, claimed a majority and were able to form a government. I swore in Sardinia on 24 November 1999 and left for Punjab the same day, my transfer orders to Punjab having arrived earlier.

Two advisors were sent to me in Goa, Coutto and Buch. On the first day of President's Rule, I went to the secretariat at 9 a.m. and found none of the staff at their desks. After 11 am some of them trickled in. I read out the 'Riot Act', and thereafter the staff began attending to their duties on time. I visited offices and institutions throughout the state, ranging from hospitals, bus services, panchayats, to schools and colleges. Corruption in Goa was rampant; so I attempted to curb it. Previously ministers appointed drivers, forest guards, and others. It was alleged that there was a fixed number for each type of appointment. I appointed a retired IAS officer as chairman of the State Public Services Commission and a retired rear admiral as his deputy and gave the commission full powers to make all appointments. The day after President's Rule expired, the government passed orders for appointments to be made in the way that had been done prior to the imposition of President's Rule, and both the chairman of the Public Services Commission and his deputy retired shortly afterwards.

The finances of the state were deeply in the red and loans were taken out at high interest rates. I managed to secure a grant from the Centre and through a series of cost-cutting measures we were able to pay back these high interest loans. When President's Rule expired there was a substantial credit balance in the treasury. It, however, took just a month for the next elected government to get once more into the 'red'!

I was appalled by the vast environmental damage caused by irresponsible open cast mining. Deep scars were visible in the western ghats and the rivers ran red, some of the smaller streams disappearing altogether. From childhood I loved the hills, the forests, fauna and flora. The mining companies who had obtained leases from the erstwhile Portuguese government had promised to fill in the scars and replant trees. They did neither.

There were two large private forests at Mhadel and Netravali (some 208.59 sq km and 211.59 sq km respectively). During President's Rule, I decided to notify these as Protected Forests so that the forests of the western ghats would be protected from end to end, and also the animals, particularly bison. The fauna and flora of Goa is unique as also the lepidoptera. I was helped in this project by the conservator of forests, Richard D'Souza, together with the Bombay Natural History Society (BNHS). We attempted to exclude all the villages, and in the end only one small village remained in the area to be notified and measures were taken to protect the interests of its villagers. There was much opposition from the mining companies, who also influenced some of the officers on my staff. The ordinance to be issued was finally ready to for signature by me a few days before the expiry of President's Rule. The chief secretary kept delaying proceedings, and in the end I was with difficulty able to wrest the file from him and sign it a few hours before the expiry of President's Rule. It was indeed a 'very close run thing'.

The politicians and the mining companies were up in arms. They approached the Supreme Court to have it rescinded but with no success. Some years later, the BJP chief minister Manohar Parrikar, who was earlier happy that the ordinance was notified, later tried to get it revoked. He approached the Supreme Court but with no success. Hopefully the forests, fauna, flora, and lepidoptora will remain protected for all time to come. The promulgation of the ordinance is perhaps among the most valuable contributions I have made in my life. Tigers have now crossed into these forests.

During this period in May 1999, there were some incursions on the bare Kargil ridges in northern J&K. The Pakistanis had employed over five battalions of their lightly equipped Northern Light Infantry. We were taken by surprise. The army chief, on tour in Europe, when briefed decided to extend his tour. As a soldier I remember one of Napoleon's maxims to his marshals, 'When in doubt march to the sound of the guns'. There were some four incursions, two some 15 kilometres by 5 and two lesser ones, spread over a limited front of some 140 kilometres or so.

I was asked by the government to go to Kargil and report back to them. I spent two days there and was briefed at the helipad as were other visiting VIPs. I went to the gun position and other front line positions. In one area the guns were engaging targets and I asked to fire the 155 mm Bofors gun and the 130 mm artillery piece. The gunners wanted to engage Skardu, but this was beyond the range of the Bofors gun. Kargil was a classic gunner's war, and it was the Bofors gun that played a pivotal role and dominated the battlefield. We deployed 250 guns and some 250,000 rounds were fired! Ninety per cent of the casualties on both sides were caused by artillery fire. The officers told me that they were running out of 155mm artillery ammunition. The adjacent area was being shelled and two Gurkhas were wounded. I took them in the helicopter to the military hospital for treatment. The JCO, severely wounded, held my hand throughout the trip, saying 'Sahib, please don't leave my hand'. He survived after a series of operations lasting over three days. We deployed some 30,000 regular and paramilitary forces, and these were supported by our air force.

I went to see Vajpayee to brief him, and he called George Fernandes to listen. I told him that the army wanted to shell Skardu, the principal Pakistani base which was out of range. The weapon system that could meet our requirements was the Russian 'Smerch', which had a range of 90 kilometres. They agreed and action was initiated to induct the Smerch. It took five years to do so because the babus in the government found all manner of reasons to delay its induction: single vendor, etc. Fortunately the Smerch, despite the delay, is in service today. I mentioned that the guns were running out of 155mm ammunition. Fernandes took immediate action and the ammunition was flown in by Israel. I took the opportunity to press for, as I had been doing for years, to improve the route to Ladakh from Himachal Pradesh via Manali, Rohtang, and Leh. This I had suggested to Advani earlier, and he told me that he had discussed the matter with Farooq Abdulla, the chief minister who had told him that 'The road was not necessary'. Did he expect any other answer? Vajpayee said the he would issue orders to have work initiated on the Rohtang tunnel.

I told Vajpayee and Fernandes that the operations in Kargil had not been well executed. There was a failure of intelligence, the patrolling and surveillance by the army had left much to be desired notwithstanding the availability of sufficient helicopters for surveillance. There was no reason why the air force should not have been used more aggressively. It was fortunate that American President Bill Clinton exerted pressure on the Pakistanis to withdraw. The BJP claimed that it was a major war that they had won. It was hardly a war: just four minor incursions over a stretch of some 140 kilometres of barren hillsides by five battalions of Pakistani paramilitary could by no means be classified as a 'great victory'.

I earlier mentioned that I installed a new government in Goa and left on 24 November 1999 to take over as governor of Punjab. A tempestuous tenure had come to an end. Interestingly, just before I left Goa, people took out processions requesting that there should not be any elections and there should be indefinite President's Rule. The BJP national executive was meeting in Goa and petitioned the prime minister, home minister, and election commissioner that they did not want elections but that President's Rule should not be revoked. Advani jokingly used to say, 'Gen Jacob is not good for democracy; people don't want elections but Jacob's rule'. (App.: Editorial Goa.)

The Punjab Tenure

I have had long pleasant association with Punjab. I had served with and commanded a Punjabi Mussalman battery for five years during the Second World War and served with the Sikh Patiala Mountain Battery. I raised 3 Field Regiment, an all-Sikh unit. When on leave I used to visit the villages of the soldiers and spend time with their families.

Raj Bhawan was located in a bungalow designed by Jennaret, one of Corbusier's assistants. The Raj Bhawan projected to be built is yet to be built, and with due respects to Corbusier would have been far too pretentious. I was fortunate in having a competent secretary, Subodh Agarwal. The staff at Raj Bhawan was loyal and efficient. The responsibilities of a governor towards a state are largely ceremonial. He may advise the chief minister as and when he deems it to be necessary.

The chief minister, when I assumed governership, was Prakash Singh Badal of the Akali Dal. We got on well. His nephew, Manpreet Singh Badal, was an intellectual and we had many long discussions. I visited towns, villages, colleges, and schools throughout the state and made suggestions to the chief minister.

Punjab's economy is agriculture-based yet the infrastructure, particularly relating to storage, is less than satisfactory. There are inadequate storage facilities and grain lies rotting under tarpaulins. There is an acute want of cold storage facilities and insufficient food processing units and marketing arrangements.

There are serious power shortages in the state and inadequate water for irrigation. The sub-soil water levels are at dangerously low levels. Earlier, the principal crop was wheat, but now both rice and wheat are sown. Rice cultivation is water intensive so there is an urgent need to diversify into other crops. There are a number of small-scale industries largely centred around Ludhiana.

There was wide-scale corruption. Appointments made by the public services were said to be sold. The chairman of the commission was later prosecuted. Badal was followed as chief minister by Capt. Amarinder Singh of the Congress Party. We got on well. Amarinder was competent and popular. However, his close advisors did little to assist him.

The Governor of Punjab is also the administrator of the Union Territory of Chandigarh, a full time assignment. My predecessors undertook their responsibilities as administrator from Raj Bhawan.

I went to the administrator's office in the secretariat and found it in a decrepit state, awash with cobwebs and dust-laden furniture! I operated out of my office there.

As in Goa, I had a blitz on the attendance of the staff and undertook surprise checks by day and night on police stations, fire brigades, schools and colleges. The fire brigades were in an appalling state with less than 50 per cent of the fire tenders in a serviceable condition.

I was fortunate in having to work with Renuka Muttoo of the Intelligence Bureau and Bhim Bassi, inspector general (IG) of police, both outstanding officers. We revamped the hotels owned by the Chandigarh Administrations CITCO, and reinducted the surplus staff into new restaurants. CITCO now runs at a considerable profit.

We were short of 550 teachers. Fortunately, Dr Murli Manohar Joshi, minister of human resource development, sanctioned 550 teachers and we ensured that they were appointed only after written examinations and follow-up interviews. We had the engineering college upgraded to deemed university and built another engineering college.

In order to give slum children, who perforce had to work by day, an education, we began night classes for these children in all the government schools. Some of them were awarded scholarships and went on to pursue higher studies. Mr Atul Khanna runs four of these schools.

Slums were a burgeoning problem. The daily influx of people from Rajasthan, UP, Bihar, as also from the south was considerable. We tried to alleviate the appalling conditions that obtained there by providing clean drinking water, building latrines, and setting up dispensaries. Tuberculosis (TB) was rampant so we set up a new TB hospital to treat the growing numbers of patients. We expanded the facilities of the hospitals, particularly the newly built Government Medical College. In the space of three years we were able to build some 2000 apartments for slum dwellers and these were allotted just after I left.

We also started a hospice, the only one in northern India, and constructed a proper botanical garden with a large variety of trees from India and abroad, which included a section on medicinal plants. We had hoped to set up laboratories in conjunction with the private sector, and linked up the 180-acre garden by a causeway with 350 acres natural forest on the outskirts of Chandigarh. The entire complex consists of some 530 acres.

I remember when I was posted to Punjab, people used to make wisecracks about Chandigarh: that it was a place where 'People went for marriages or funerals'; it was a city where very little happened. When I arrived, restaurants and bars were shut down at 10 p.m. This we extended to 1 am. Later I met the commissioner of police who before I arrived, was responsible for this. I was informed that the reason was to prevent the young taking to drugs. I retorted that what this implied was that the young people would not take drugs during the day but only during the hours between 10 p.m. and 1 p.m. The individual was not amused and walked off in a huff.

There were very few avenues for employment, particularly for the young graduates from the many schools and colleges in the city and very little land available for development. There were 118 acres of land on the outskirts that were earmarked for a polluting power station. I decided to allot this land for an IT Park. IT companies were reluctant to come to Chandigarh, so I made two trips to Bangalore, Chennai, and Hyderabad to try to persuade them to do so. I met executives from Infosys, Satyam, and Wipro, and managed to persuade Narayan Murthy of Infosys to set up a complex at Chandigarh; Wipro and Satyam declining. A memo of understanding was signed by H.R. Binod of Infosys and Karan Avtar Singh, finance secretary of the Chandigarh administration, on 15 November 2002. The agreement was entirely due to the pragmatism of Murthy who, notwithstanding the reluctance of some of his subordinates to set up shop in Chandigarh, told them 'I have given my word to Gen. Jacob and we will keep it'. Today, Infosys is flourishing in Chandigarh. With the coming of Infosys, other IT companies soon followed, making it an IT hub. Real-estate prices have soared and employment avenues have opened up for young graduates from the colleges and schools.

In my travels around the world, in the US, the UK, Russia, and the Philippines, I have seen how these countries honour their dead. I was most impressed by the memorial at Leningrad (Saint Petersburg).

At the end of the 1971 war, Manekshaw wanted to immediately set up a memorial. I suggested the First World War memorial at India Gate, gave him a sketch, and sent a rifle, bayonet, and helmet that belonged to an unknown soldier who had laid down his life in the battle for Jessore.

I wanted a memorial for those in the erstwhile Punjab, Haryana, Himachal, and Chandigarh. I was not being able to raise the money when an old friend and editor of the *Indian Express* offered to do so. I approached the students of the Architectural College, Chandigarh, to design the monument.

Some twelve teams were formed. I gave them a brief to work on. The designs of the proposed memorial were submitted to veterans for selection and the one finally selected was by a group of girls. The memorial was inaugurated by President Dr A.P.J. Abdul Kalam on 17 August 2006. While I was addressing the audience on the sacrifices made by our soldiers, the governor began engaging the president in chatter and the president responded. This was a solemn occasion in honour of our war dead I could take it no longer. I turned from the dais and looked at the president and said, 'Mr President'. He took the hint and focused on what I had to say. The incident was widely reported by the media. I had the motto of the memorial of 26 Indian Division in the Arakan '*Shandaar Yadgaar*', two words which have much resonance, adopted for this memorial. One day I hope some government will come to power which will construct a national memorial for all those who laid down their lives for India. I am reminded of the oldest epitaph commemorating Leonidas and his Spartans at Thermopylae in 480 BC: 'Go tell the Spartans, O stranger passing by, that here obedient to their laws we lie' (Simonizes of Ceos, poet, 556 to 468 BC).

When I was appointed governor of Goa, I resigned from the BJP, because a governor must be apolitical. Most governors don't resign. Unfortunately, the local political leaders felt that I had an obligation to go out of my way to help them in their various activities. One local BJP leader came to see me and had the audacity to tell me that before announcing any policy or initiative I should call him three days prior to pronouncing it and to brief him. I did little to conceal my ire and he soon beat a hasty retreat. He then wrote to the prime minister, home minister, and others that I was not helping the party but rather favouring a rival one. This gentleman brings to mind the old adage, 'Politics is the last refuge of a scoundrel'.

I felt for the poor, the underprivileged, the slum dwellers, pavement dwellers, and cycle-rickshaw pullers. I would venture out at night and distribute blankets, especially on New Year's Eve, when the elite were partying at clubs, hotels, restaurants, and homes. I have had blankets and food snatched from my hands. On these visits I had medical teams, doctors, and ambulances follow me. The number of TB cases diagnosed, treated, and sent for further treatment was alarming. Rather than supporting these forays, one editor of a newspaper wrote that Lt Gen. Jacob was breaking the law by giving blankets to 'illegal pavement dwellers'.

I look back to my tenure in Chandigarh with a sense of achievement. Perhaps the finest tribute I have ever received was one reported by some newspapers, some six months after I demitted office, there was, scrawled on the walls of hospitals and elsewhere, this slogan: 'Now that Jacob has gone, who will look after the poor?'! What better endorsement could one ask for?

Visit to the US

In 2007, the Indian American community requested me to lecture in America to push for the 123 Agreement. I lectured in nine American cities, and these lectures were well attended. The Indian American community were keen to hear about the operations for the liberation of Bangladesh.

In order to lobby for the 123 Agreement, I arranged on my own to meet the various heads of the powerful Congressional committees involved. I had an hour-long meeting with the late Congressman Tom Lantos, who had earlier been lukewarm about the treaty but after the meeting, promised his support. Howard Berman was more difficult but also agreed to lend his support. I had two separate meetings with Ileana Ros-Lehtinen, the second at her request, in the course of which she too promised her support. I also met Congressman Ackerman who also promised his support, as did Senator Joe Lieberman. Apart from Ileana Ros-Lehtinen, who is a republican, the rest are democrats. I received no support from the Indian embassy, and am told that they were not very enthusiastic about my meetings. The people I met readily gave me time but interestingly they were not easily accessible to members of our mission or visiting politicians.

I met with the top brass of the American Jewish Committee (AJC) in four cities to enlist their support. The AJC has enormous clout with the American administration and promised their support.

I lectured on Capitol Hill to select members of the US military and state departments. The subject was 'Terrorism and Insurgency' and the lecture was broadcast live. The general of the marine corps asked for a copy of my lecture and requested that he be permitted to include parts of it in their manual on terrorism and insurgent conflicts that was under preparation. I naturally agreed.

Later, when I met the prime minister, I was a little surprised that he was unaware of my efforts; presumably they had not been reported by our embassy, who were not amused.

13

Some Abiding Impressions

When I look back on my journey through life I realize that it was indeed tempestuous. My school days were not the happiest, as a couple of British teachers nurtured some anti-Semitism, but I was able to cope with that. On the other hand, the Jewish community in India has never experienced any anti-Semitism from fellow Indians. The Jewish community has prospered in India for some 2000 years. My days in the army were eventful and I was the only Indian officer in the regiment the others being British. I had no problems when I joined the regiment because its officers were from the upper crust of British society and true gentlemen. As the war progressed, officers of different social status joined. Later, towards the end of the war, a few Indian officers joined the regiment. One of them was Shaukat Reza, my second-in-command. He later commanded the Pakistani 9 Infantry Division in East Pakistan. When I knew Shaukat he was a caring officer. Anthony Masceranas (the well-known news correspondent) had alleged that the 9 Infantry Division that he commanded was responsible for the largest number of atrocities. Shaukat was moved in October 1971 to GHQ to become director general of military operations, Pakistan Army. My experiences of working with British officers were for the most part cordial. If you knew your job they gave you your due. I remember in Burma, as a young captain, my battery commander, Dick Peters, patting me on my back during a particular operation with the words: 'Jacko, your reward will be in heaven.'

I was fortunate in the Arakan, as a major, to get to know Lt Col Cariappa, Lt Col Thimayya, Lt Col L.P. (Bogey) Sen, Lt Col S.P.P. Thorat, and Maj. Bikram Singh. Later, when we returned to India, I remained a major until 1956. The others had after Independence shot up to the ranks of general officers, taking their seniority from the date of their commissions.

Army life is tough. One has sometimes to serve under pompous and ambitious bullies. I had problems with some of them. One had to stand tall and not bend. I had the ill fortune to serve under Maj. Gen. 'Bijji' Kaul in the 4 Infantry Division. Kaul had the political backing of Defence Minister Krishna Menon. Kaul tried to 'recruit' me into his coterie of confidantes to further his military and possibly political ambitions.

Great pressure was exerted on me to bend to his wishes. At one point I even thought of resigning. Fortunately, Gen. Kumaramangalam heard of this and had me posted out. Some years later Kaul phoned me at the Staff College to give evidence against General Manekshaw at an enquiry instituted to examine his anti-national activities. Kaul threatened me, saying that if I did not cooperate my career would be in jeopardy. I still declined. True to his word, Kaul had my name moved from the top of the promotion list to the bottom. Years later, when Kaul retired after his incompetent handling of the 1962 war, he was in Delhi, heartbroken and shunned, I went to see him. Tears streaming down his cheeks, he said, 'Jacob, of all people you have come to see me'. I said, 'General you were once my GOC. Do please let me know if I can help in any way.' He did not respond and I left him in tears. Such is life. Later, as a brigadier, when I was commandant, Artillery School, I had problems with Maj. Gen. Naravane who had once been a fellow prisoner of war of Kumaramangalam. The experience had, it is said, affected his mental balance. He wanted me to pass the 75mm mountain gun for which he was project-in-charge and had come for trials. The gun had over 90 defects, some of them major, so I refused. He gave me a low average annual confidential report. This notwithstanding, I was promoted to command a division and had the good fortune to serve under Lt Gen. Moti Sagar, who was then Southern Army Commander. Moti had been my platoon commander and thus my immediate officer, instructor when I was a cadet. 12 Infantry Division which I commanded came directly under Moti, and he gave me a free hand and encouragement. He was a thorough gentleman.

Unfortunately, personal vendettas are on the increase. The army chief, Gen. Gopal Bewoor, phoned me when I was Eastern Army commander to say that he was posting Maj. Gen. S.K. Sinha to 23 Infantry Division and that I should 'fix' him. I did not respond. Some time later Manekshaw, on one of his many trips to Calcutta to attend company board meetings, came to see me. He told me that Sinha was responsible to Gen. Kaul for orchestrating the inquiry against him in 1961 and that I should fix him. I did not like being told to do what I felt was not correct. I ensured that as I had been told to fix Sinha, he would get a good confidential report. When Bewoor received it he phoned me and asked why I had given him a good report, and the basis on which I had initiated it when Sinha had not even completed a year under me. I replied that according to regulations an army commander can initiate a report on any officer at any time. I added that if he wrote adverse comments and if Sinha appealed I would quote this conversation. Sinha was later cleared for promotion.

Not only was Bewoor wanting to *fix* officers, so also was Gen. 'Tappy' Raina. Raina had phoned me to fix Lt Gen. Stan Menezes who was then commanding IV Corps under me. Raina said that Menezes was fit only for the staff and unfit to command an army, and that I should not recommend him for the post of army commander. I told him that Menezes was a competent officer and that I would be recommending him for that rank. He thereupon retorted that he would not pass him as army commander but on the staff as vice chief, equivalent to the rank of army commander. Later he phoned me regarding the recently promoted Lt Gen. W.A.G. Pinto, and said that I should fix him. I replied that he as army chief had cleared Pinto for promotion to the rank of Lt General when he was his director of military training. I said I would not fix Pinto and was not prepared to be used. Pinto was later cleared for the rank of army commander.

I owe a great deal to Gen. Kumaramangalam. He took a liking to me from our days at the Artillery School. Later I was his staff officer at the Artillery Directorate. He trusted me completely and gave me a free hand. When I took a number of policy decisions and signed policy letters, the master general of ordnance, Lt Gen. Sant Singh wanted my scalp when I was moving to do a course at the Staff College. Kumaramanglam supported me and the action against me that Lt Gen. Sant Singh demanded, fizzled out. I indeed owe much to Kumaramangalam and was greatly saddened by his passing away.

The army I joined in 1941 has changed dramatically through the years. An army officer in those days was respected. To quote an example, in 1943 I was sent from Burma with a small detachment to collect the latest mortars for the regiment from the ordnance depot at Jabalpore. I collected the weapons and went to the railway station. There I met the station master and asked him when the next train from Jabalpore to Calcutta would leave. He said the next train was due to arrive but said it was the Calcutta Mail, but as there was no room for the mortars I would have to wait for a much slower train the next day. I asked about the mail van, but he said it was full. I said, 'Cannot you unload the mail and send it later?' impressing upon him that we needed these weapons urgently. He was sympathetic and said that he would need some authority to do so. I told him I would provide a letter of authority. He took out his pad and I wrote: 'I Capt. Jack Jacob, Royal Indian Artillery, authorize the station master, Jabalpore to unload the mail and transport weapons in its place', Jack Jacob, Capt.'. The mail was unloaded and the mortars loaded and moved rapidly to the front. This is an example of the status then enjoyed by army officers. Since 1947, the status of the army officer vis-a-vis his counterparts in the civil service and police has been steadily eroded over the years. The civil service boast that they are government but in reality they are government servants. They feel that the Mont Blanc pens they wield are more powerful than the sword. The three services remain disappointed with the sixth pay commission. Though people opting for the non-combat services has increased, the continued shortage of officers remains a matter of grave concern.

We have perhaps the best military in the world, but they require the support and appreciation of the government and the people, and modern equipment. Modern weapon systems are complex and take a long time to assimilate, and also require logistical back up. We are short of guns. After the induction of the Bofors gun, no 155mm howitzers have been bought. There are critical shortages of spares and ammunition. For example, during the Kargil incursions by some five battalions plus of Pakistan's Northern Light Infantry spread over a few kilometres of barren ridge, we ran out of 155mm ammunition and the Israelis had to fly it in.

Considering our GDP, the allocations for defence are proportionately low. Monies allotted are not fully utilized and much of it surrendered due to the inordinate delays resulting from irrational procedures.

Today, driving around Lutyen's Delhi you will see numerous guards at the residences of army generals. These guards they claim are there for reasons of security. Unless since changed, 'Regulations Army in India' authorized only one guard in a station. Even the vice chief in 1979 was not authorized a guard. The number of soldiers employed as guards and to undertake domestic chores is burgeoning, at a time when active units are short of manpower. It is time that these soldiers revert to the duties for which they were enrolled. Incredibly, the government has authorized retired service chiefs to be allotted two batmen each. Nowhere else in the world does such a provision exist.

A complaint of junior and middle-level officers is the lavish lifestyle of senior officers. It may be relevant to take an example from the UK. The chiefs of defence staff of the rank earlier of field marshal or equivalent now four-star generals, reside in a government flat in Kensington in London. There is no guard (this even during the days of IRA terrorism) and only a receptionist in the lobby. I visited some of them in earlier days. There was only one batman, and on occasion the officers served the drinks themselves.

I am impressed by our young officers. They are far better trained than I was and far better educated militarily. I had to learn my soldiering on the battlefield. Our middle piece officers are dedicated and competent. After Cariappa, Thimayya, Kumaramangalam, and Manekshaw we have not produced any army chief of any great distinction. Fortunately after many years, we have in Gen. V.K. Singh an army chief who is not only competent but commands an exemplary degree of integrity.

Today there is a parallel chain of command in the services. A wives' chain of command influence matters where they should have no locus standi. I had earlier to speak to the army chief, Raina, regarding the posting out of a commanding officer on a timeframe of 24 hours. On enquiring, the army chief told me that the wife of the second-in-command had written to his wife. I asked whether he or his wife was running the army, to which he did not reply. I told him that the posting order should be cancelled immediately or I would see the defence minister regarding the matter. He agreed to issue orders to cancel the posting (and did).

Lord Louis Mountbatten, as viceroy, had instructed that when an officer was appointed army commander, no further report would be initiated and that the army commander's dossier would then be held by the defence minister. This he did to ensure the independence of the army commander, who was a field army commander as opposed to being a 'chief of army staff'. The army chief is not a commander in chief, and is appointed from amongst the army commanders and is, under normal circumstances, the seniormost among them.

There is a need to recast and redefine our organizational and tactical doctrines. Army training manuals stipulate that defence is the basic operation of war. This is not so. The basic operation is the attack or offensive. Our organizations are tailored with this in mind. The British and some Commonwealth countries' infantry battalions have four rifle companies. This was based on British military thinking prior to and during the two world wars with weightage on defence. The Russian, American, and most other armies have three rifle companies in a battalion. It is difficult for a commanding officer to handle more than three companies in offensive operations. During my years in Burma I did not see any assault with more than one company in the assault, one in reserve, and one as part of the firm base. The only arm that has been reorganized since the Second World War is the artillery. The eight-gun battery of two troops has been reorganized as a 6-gun battery.

In September 1971, Eastern Command was provided with wheeled armoured personnel carriers (APCs) for two battalions. I was given the task to work out the establishment of the battalions as also the operating procedures. The Infantry and Staff Duties Directorates at Army HQ wanted to keep the existing organizations and to just mount the infantry in the APCs, as was the case in the old motorized battalions. I reorganized them on the lines of assault units: units of three assault companies. I streamlined the organizations, shed the platoons that were no longer relevant. Fortunately the director, military operations, Maj. Gen. Inder Gill backed me and got the reorganizations through and I wrote out the operating procedures. Thus in 1971, the mechanized infantry came into being. There was not sufficient time for training and these two battalions were not used to their full effect in the subsequent operations.

The armoured regiments too need reorganization. We have 14 tanks in a squadron, four troops of three tanks, and two in squadron HQ. This organization is based on outdated tactics. The Russians used tanks most effectively during the Second World War, thousands of T-34s being employed in battle, the Kursk being one. There are only ten tanks in a Russian company/squadron, three troops of three tanks and one for the commander. We should also rationalize our armoured regiments. Many countries are giving preference to brigade group organizations rather than the division. The armoured division was intended to be used for the breakout, that is, after the enemy defences have been breached. The division is then unleashed to strike at targets in the rear. The armoured divisions in our wars have been underutilized. Given the greater flexibility of the armoured brigade group we need to restructure our armoured formations laying emphasis on maneuverability and flexibility.

Today the greatest military threat is China. China refuses to drop its claims on Arunachal Pradesh and is building up its infrastructure including rail, roads, and airfields in Tibet. China can, in a space of some two weeks, deploy some 30 divisions in Tibet. China is of course also trying to establish control in the Indian Ocean with bases in Ramree Island and Gwadar in the Gulf of Oman.

Our infrastructure and troop strengths are less than adequate. Our mountain divisions require modern weapon systems and lack mobility, particularly troop equipment and helicopter mobility. The artillery is equipped with light howitzers. From my experience during the Second World War, only heavy shells had any effect in the mountains. There is a need for more divisions with heavier guns and more helicopters. It takes time to raise and re-equip mountain divisions.

The geopolitical and geo–military environment that obtains today is highly volatile. In the west we have Pakistan, driven by terrorism and home to many international and home-grown terrorist organizations. The Taliban is gaining control over most of the western parts of the country and is trying to gain control of Sind and southern Punjab. The ISI is stepping up its terrorist activities in Jammu & Kashmir and is establishing terrorist cells in many parts of India. It is also using Nepal and Bangladesh as surrogate jumping off areas for their terrorist activities. Bangladesh too was hosting hostile terrorists for operations in the North East and elsewhere in India. Nepal is another area of concern. The Maoist regime is moving closer to China and is reported to be establishing links with the Naxalites. To the south, the Sri Lanka campaign against the LTTE, though now at an end, is having a spill-over in the southern states.

In this volatile environment, India needs to reorganize its archaic security set up. The US established its Homeland Security and since 9/11 there have been no terrorist attacks there. There is a need to get to grips with the security of our country. We should have a proactive policy rather than a reactive one. Our attitude of 'lassiez faire' must be replaced by a pragmatic approach to national security. We should be able to speak and act from a position of strength (remember Theodore [Teddy] Roosevelt's advice: 'Speak softly but carry a big stick.').

The events of 26/11 exposed our inability to effectively counter ISI-controlled terrorist activities. Our reaction was delayed, ineffective, and pedestrian, the entire drama played out on television. It exposed our police and paramilitary forces in a very poor light.

Travels after Retirement

After retirement I visited many countries in South Africa. I met Nelson Mandela and Chief Buthelezi. In London, I met the queen of England in Saint James' Palace. Present there were Prince Phillip and the former king of Greece. In America, I had meetings with several congressmen and senators. In all these meetings I took the opportunity to lobby for India's interests in various fields.

I was invited to Israel for the 3000th anniversary of the founding of Jerusalem by Prime Minister Yitzhak Rabin. I also met my old friend Gen. Mordecai Gur, the defence minister. Rabin and Mordecai Gur were keen to get my views on a range of subjects, and these were discussed in two separate sessions.

In 2009, I was invited to attend the Maccabiah games in Tel Aviv. I took the opportunity of meeting President Shimon Peres, whom I had known over a period of many years.

In London, I had interacted with Lord Geville Janner. Janner had invited me to become a patron of the Commonwealth Jewish Council back in the 1980s. Janner set up meetings for me with many decision-makers in the UK. I also had discussions at the Institute of Strategic Studies in London and had the opportunity of meeting Tony Blair and dining with him.

I have been advocating to the authorities that they reorganize our security infrastructure using the American Homeland Security apparatus as an example. There has been no terrorist attack in the US since 9/11.

The Maoists are taking control over more and more areas and the state governments are unable to counter them. They are linking up too with anti-Indian elements in Nepal, the North East, and Bangladesh. In 1969, Indira Gandhi ordered the army to deal with the Naxalites in West Bengal and they were driven out by mid 1971. Indira Gandhi had a pragmatic approach. If the army was used from 1969 to 1971 to crush the Naxalites, why then is the government now so reluctant to use it? Very recently (March–April 2010), following some particularly vicious Maoist attacks on paramilitary forces and civilians, the Government of India began seriously considering the use of trained armed forces to tackle the menace. In the 6 April Dantewada incident (Chhattisgarh) some 77 paramilitary personnel were killed in an ambush. Subsequently a splinter group of the Maoists derailed a Mumbai bound train near Jhagram (West Midnapore district in West Bengal) killing over 60 innocent civilians and injuring over 200, creating a national furore in press and parliament. Let us hope that better judgement prevails before the situation gets completely out of control.

Finally, my innings is nearing its end. It has been a tempestuous journey. I tried my best to do my duty as a soldier. As a governor, despite pressures, I tried to be apolitical and impartial. I recall lines from a poem by Gerard Manley Hopkins:

> For I have desired to be in fields where springs not fail,
> Where flies no deep and sided hail,
> And a few lilies blow.
> Those fields lie near and beckon.

Hic finis fandi

Appendix 1: Excerpts from Letters to the Author

Gen. Kumaramangalam (retd), Tamil Nadu
1 August 1978

In regard to what you did for the army, this I hope will be written down in history. You were kind enough the give me an idea of what your plans were and the speed of the operations in Bangladesh was entirely due to your imaginative plans. Speed was essential then and you did this in spite of orders otherwise from above. I hope from the lessons of the operations, the army will understand that mobility is an important principle of war – I always felt that Monty was wrong … substitution of flexibility for mobility as a principle of war. Certainly the Indian Army should give more attention to mobility.

Governor, Assam, Raj Bahavan, Shillong
10 August 1978

In your retirement, you are entitled to have the feeling that you had made outstanding contributions, first to restoration, and then to maintenance of peace, in the parts of the north-eastern region which had suffered from insurgency for long periods. This could be possible only by an extraordinary combination of knowledge, high competence, and identification with the larger interests of the country. So many holders of high offices, in the armed forces, or civil administration, tend to keep things going somehow rather than show any initiative or take risks.

Rano Shaiza, Member of Parliament
Lok Sabha
New Delhi 30 December 1977

I would like to mention on behalf of the Naga people, whom I represent in Parliament, our appreciation of the change in attitude that you were able to bring about in the army in Nagaland. I know that you, more than anyone else, have done your best to truly project the security forces as the champions of peace who are also interested in the welfare of the people of the state in which they are stationed. So, you will now find the Nagas thinking less and less in terms of blame and more in appreciation of your efforts. May I thank you once again for the goodness you have been generating in this small corner of the country.

Maj. Gen. D.K. Palit, VrC,
New Delhi, 5 May 2007

The general impression in Delhi (probably influenced by what Army HQ under Sam's influence was putting out) was that it was Sam who had resisted pressures from Mrs Gandhi and the ministry to go into the offensive in Bangladesh immediately. I see from the *Hindu* interview that on the contrary Sam wanted a premature offensive with limited aims – and it was you who held out for restraint and to wait to attack only when the strategic, tactical, and logistical factors (and the international climate) offered the Indians optimum conditions. To one who had the opportunity of sizing up Sam's pro-British and anti-Indian shallow character, that sounds entirely in accordance. (Just to give one example: he gave himself the sobriquet of 'Sam Bahadur', talked endlessly about the Gorkhas – but in fact never served in any Gorkha Regiment)....

During my DMO-ship, Manekshaw was commandant, Staff College. He was sent for by Army HQ to face a Court of Inquiry for anti-Indian statements he made to British and other foreign students at the college. Lt Gen. Daulat Singh was the chairman and

he let him off lightly – Bijji Kaul was the CGS who had instituted the inquiry (and Daulat was not exactly a fan of Bijji Kaul!).
Do keep in touch
Yours sincerely,
D.K. Palit

General K.V. Krishna Rao, PVSM (retd)
Secunderabad 500094
July 2005
I have now read your book from cover to cover and I feel compelled to write to you.

I personally feel that it is a comprehensive, candid, and truthful account of the war, as you saw it. There were many things that we did not know about, particularly the firm and tactful way you handled Niazi before the surrender ceremony. The manner in which you dealt with extremely difficult situations before and during the war, brings out the originality, moral courage and sense of national strategic commitment that you displayed. My heartiest congratulations to you on this excellent effort.

I consider that you played a very significant role in the achievement of our glorious victory in the 1971 war. You have indeed gone up in the esteem and respect that I have for you.
With warm regards and God be with you,
Krishna Rao

Lt Gen. Moti Sagar, PVSM
Director General, Civil Defence, Ministry of Home Affairs
17 December 1971
My dear Jake,
The enemy has been defeated in battle and has surrendered; that our forces moved so rapidly and so completely enveloped and surrounded the enemy with such speed is in a very great measure due to your brilliant planning and excellent staff work. You have worked patiently, calmly, and incessantly to make the operation a success. In spite of many handicaps, you gave much encouragement to the formation commanders and others with your quiet but unchallenged efficiency and were a source of inspiration to them.

Yours sincerely,
Moti Sagar

Signal from Gen. Candeth addressed to me and not Aurora
Gen. Candeth was Western Army Commander and was in close touch with events
Personal
For Maj. Gen. Jacob from Candeth...
'Congratulations on your victory and your part in negotiating enemy's surrender.'

Lt Gen. I.S. Gill (Retd.)
South Bank Road, Madras-800028, 18 May 1997

My Dear Jake,
When I read of your first interview for a commission by a board of officers clad in gabardine I chuckled as I thought back to the Middle East during the war when we called the regulars on the staff of GHQ the 'Gabardine Swine'.

Congratulations, Jake. You have written a very good and readable book (very important for the general public) which adequately emphasizes all the points you consider need emphasis. I think you have filled in all the blanks, without fear or favour.

Yours Sincerely
I.S. Gill

Appendix 2: Excerpts from Media and other Documents

HERALD
Panjim, 30 November 1989
A Tribute to General Jacob

Lt Gen. Jacob, a nominee of the BJP-led alliance government presided over the destiny of the state during one of the most turbulent periods in Goa's political history. The tenure of Lt Gen. Jacob was marred by an epidemic of defections and counter defections which saw a succession of very short-lived governments. It started with the collapse of the Pratapsing Rane-led Congress government following the revolt by Dr Wilfred de Souza and culminated with the swearing in of the Congress–Bharatiya Janata Party coalition government headed by Francisco Sardinha. This was the last constitutional duty enforced by Lt. General Jacob before he relinquished his office. All through the political turbulence that rocked Goa during the current year, the Governor, Lt Gen. Jacob earned the respect of all the political groups in the state by his strict neutrality. The Governor, Lt Gen. Jacob very strictly adhered to the rules and norms set by the Constitution. President's rule was imposed in the State earlier this year when it became clear that no party or group was in position to form the Government.

The duration of President's rule during which Lt General Jacob not only reigned but also ruled was the high point of his tenure as Governor of the State. Lt General Jacob demonstrated and dramatized the fact that jumbo cabinets were not necessary and the Sate could be administered very efficiently by just a team of three. Comprising the governor and his two advisers when Lt. General Jacob inherited the responsibility of taking charge of the administration of the State, the economy was in shambles and the State was virtually bankrupt. To make matters worse, the popular government that had preceded the imposition of President's rule in the State had behaved in a most irresponsible manner and had resorted to borrowing large sums of money from the Economic Development Corporation and the cooperative banks at very high rates of interest. The administration in the State had come virtually to a standstill because of chronic political instability and the succession of governments.

Lt General Jacob rose magnificently to the new challenge before him. Lt General Jacob adopted a hands-on style of governance with a total commitment to the ordinary citizens of the State. Lt General Jacob enforced discipline in the State administration by setting an example himself. During his tenure as Administrator, Lt General Jacob arrived on time or even before time at the Adil Shah Palace housing the Secretariat, compelling senior and junior bureaucrats to arrive in time. Lt General Jacob made surprise visits to both the North and South Goa Collectorates and even the Goa Medical College and the Kadamba Bus Stand at Panjim to tone up the administration. The administrator made himself freely accessible to ordinary citizens at the Secretariat and made sure that the bureaucrats promptly attended to the grievances of the people. Corruption was totally eliminated during Lt General Jacob's tenure as administrator. Among his major achievements was the fact that being a lover of nature he created two additional sanctuaries in the State by ruthlessly cutting down on wasteful expenditure.

Lt General Jacob strengthened the financial position of the State to the extent that some of the high interest loans were paid back. The governor using his close contact with senior Bharatiya Janata Party leaders managed to secure an additional grant of Rs Fifty crore to strengthen the administration. Lt General Jacob specifically allotted funds for strengthening various infrastructural facilities like power, water supply, transport and improving medical facilities at the Goa Medical College. In response to demands and places from the tourism industry, the governor successfully interceded with the then Defence Minister George Fernandes to permit night landing facilities at the Navy controlled Dabolim Airport. This has enabled more charters to land in Goa. The governor also took a keen interest in preserving historical monuments and the heritage of Goa. Lt General Jacob led a very simple life and was very conscious of the need to cut down expenditures when the he went to London to attend a Commonwealth-sponsored meeting of non-governmental bodies. He paid his fare and made his own arrangements for accommodation and did not impose any burden on the State.

The most notable aspect of Lt General Jacob's tenure as a governor was that he acted in totally non-partisan manner in dealing with the various political crises that occurred during his tenure. The governor went strictly by the Constitution in dealing with the claims and the counter claims made by various political practices in the State. During the brief span of President's rule in the State, he demonstrated that he was a very able and efficient administrator. Indeed, the ordinary citizens were so happy that there were even demands that Presidential rule should be extended. But being a staunch democrat, the governor went back to his rule as head of the state when elections were held and a popular government reinstalled in the State. Of all the governors who served in Goa, Lt General Jacob was the best by any yardstick. The people of Goa owe Lt General Jacob a great debt of gratitude for genuine commitment and dedication to the people of Goa.

Excerpt from *Crossed Swords* By Shuja Nawaz, Oxford Publishers, 2008

In the words of a later Pakistan National Defence study of the war, 'the Indians planned and executed their offensive against East Pakistan in a textbook manner. It was a classic example of thorough planning, minute coordination and bold execution.'[45] The credit clearly goes to General Jacob's meticulous preparations in the Indian eastern command and to the implementation by his corps commanders, like Tappy Raina in West Bengal who improved in the field and kept the momentum going … they managed to isolate Pakistani defenders in their separate sectors, bypassing tough targets and hitting them from the rear.

Appendix 3: Memorandum of Conversation filed by Mr Hitchcock, Consul General Calcutta, to US Department of State, 15 October 1966

Excerpt of Conversation between Lt Gen. S.H.F.J. Manekshaw, GOC-in-C Eastern Command and Mr Hitchcock on 12 October

MEMORANDUM OF CONVERSATION

Returning by Indian Airlines from New Delhi to Calcutta the night of October 12, I had the opportunity of having an uninterrupted two-hour conversation with General Manekshaw. He seemed less guarded than during any of the many talks we have had over the past two years.

1. **India and Pakistan:** As he had done with Ambassador Bowles in Calcutta a month ago, the General emphasized his conviction that the resolution of Indo-Pak differences in the central challenge confronting the two countries. The key to the difficulty in Kashmir, and he is hopeful that a new and basic reexamination of this problem can be undertaken immediately

after the Indian elections in February 1967. The continuance of Indo-Pak differences forces each country to fritter away its relatively limited resources on efforts to maintain adequate protection against the eventuality of open conflict. The Indo-Pak border should be much like the US–Canadian border, and the defence policies of the two countries should be common rather than opposed. Together they could provide the force necessary to counter China without assistance from others. He remains confident that Ayub has few illusions about China but finds himself in a political box, incapable of pressing his views even on his own people. In the formulation of a negotiating position on Kashmir, Manekshaw believes the Indian military and the civil servants can make a much more significant contribution than they have in the past. Heretofore India's posture frequently has been determined by domestic political considerations at odds with the strategic realities the two countries confront in Asia.

2. **The September 1965 Indo–Pak War.** Although he said he realizes that hindsight is of little value, he speculated ruminatingly that a number of basic problems would probably have been settled to the long range benefit of all had the September 1965 war gone on for two or three months more. He said he was at that time in daily contact with the Indian Army Chief of Staff, General Chaudhuri, and had argued vigorously against the inhibitions India imposed upon itself in order to avoid encouraging Chinese intercession into the war. He told Chaudhuri that he did not believe the Chinese would move but said he would heartily welcome such an attack and was confident this would be the most effective, possibly the only, way to explode the Indian 'myth' of Chinese invincibility. It was ridiculous, he said, that the Indian allowed the Chinese, through a few menacing sounds, to pin down the more than <u>300,000 troops he has in his command.</u> (This is the first time he has ever mentioned such a figure to me, though it is consistent with our previous assumptions.) He was quite critical of Chaudhuri's conduct of the war, contending that the Chief of Staff, a victim of the numbers game, was excessively conscious of how many Patton tanks he had destroyed in the last engagement without knowing precisely why he was destroying

them in the first place. He also differed with the Indian secretive attitude toward both the Indian and foreign press. He said that few countries have a more limited capacity of projecting themselves to the world in a favorable light than India.

3. **Indian Military 1962-66**. This last point led to my asking him why India doesn't make available to the press of the world information which would show the dramatic contrast between its strength now and its weakness in 1962, particularly as this strength constitutes an inescapably important consideration in any Chinese calculation with regard to the subcontinent. A greater realization by India that they are as committed as they are against China might lead to a more realistic attitude on their part toward Vietnam. He replied that he wished I had asked the question a month ago, i.e. before he went to Delhi to substitute for the Indian Army Chief of Staff during the latter's recent visit to Moscow. While Manekshaw was in Delhi he had many opportunities for 'brutally frank' discussions with Defence Minister Chavan, and he would have been delighted to have advocated such a line of action. However, now he would have to go through the Chief of Staff and, as with the previous Chief of Staff, he finds it difficult to press for a course of action which might be difficult to sell to India's political leadership. He said he was nevertheless going to look into this question.
4. I asked him whether he had any further thoughts about when he might be able to go to the states. (I and others had broached this subject with him several times in the past and he had always put us off by saying he couldn't possibly leave his command for the required period of time.) His reply to the question this time was most interesting. 'If they select me as Chief of Staff (implying by his tone that the expected this to occur), I would be delighted to go.' He said he was deeply concerned over the degree to which India is becoming militarily dependent to Soviet equipment. This dependence has developed out of arrangements made during discussions Chaudhuri and, more recently, Kumaramangalam had held with the Soviets in Moscow; discussions which, he added, are producing a lot of equipment for India. He believes that if he were to go to the US now the consequences would be

(1) that he would be identified with a Western bias (which he most definitely has), (2) that such identification might thwart his promotion to Chief of Staff, and (3) that not being Chief of Staff, he would be unable to take effective action to redirect Indian military thinking away from the Soviet Union. I said that I found all this most interesting; I felt that I could assure him a welcome in the US whenever he thought it might be propitious to go.

Appendix 4: US Releases Bangladesh Minutes: 15 August 1975

Daily News Monitoring Service

After killing of Bangabandhu Sheikh Mujibur Rahman on August 15, 1975 Khandoker Mushtaque Ahmed government was worried about possible Indian military intervention in Bangladesh. David Corn, US Consul General posted in Calcutta was instructed by US secretary of state Dr Henry Kissinger to keep watch on General Jacob, the chief of the Indian Eastern Command. US Ambassador in Dhaka, Davis Booster, said US Calcutta-based Consul General David Corn was adequately briefed in this regard... (*The New Nation*).

The just-released Bangladesh minutes of the US Foreign Ministry revealed that in a meeting in Calcutta on August 16, 1975, Gen. Jacob asked US Consul Corn what more he had on the Bangladesh situation? Corn said, coup in Bangladesh was successful. Gen. Jacob retorted, he had information that there were some disturbances outside Dhaka. Jacob said, Bangladesh had least chance of attaining stability, adding there was still a possibility of counter-coup. He expressed his concern over declaration of Bangladesh as Islamic republic. When Gen Jacob was asked whether there was exodus of minority Hindus from Bangladesh, he parried the question and said they were watching the situation. David Corn said that he again met Jacob on August 24 at Fort William, the headquarters of Eastern Command....

Jacob told Corn that the then President of Bangladesh, Khandoker Mushtaque, was known in India as pro-Pakistani and pro-Chinese.

Appendix 5: The March of Naxalism

The Naxal movement was born in the little thatch-hut village of Naxalbari in north Bengal around 1967. The movement spread and soon became a serious threat to governance in the state. As the police could not handle the situation, the then Prime Minister Mrs Indira Gandhi took a pragmatic decision in October 1969 to use the army.

Army Chief Sam Manekshaw and secretary to the goverment Govind Narayan, met me in Fort William, the Eastern Command Headquarters. They told me that since the police were unable to handle the Naxals, the army would have to do so. I told Manekshaw that it was not the army's job, and that the police should try harder.

Manekshaw then said that the police were unable to deal with the situation, and therefore Mrs Gandhi had directed that the army should be assigned the task, and that I was to be put in charge of the operations.

I then informed Manekshaw that though we had 20 Infantry Division near Naxalbari, we did not have sufficient troops south of the Ganga. I asked for two more divisions. Done, said Manekshaw, adding that he would be good to me and also allot the 50 Para Brigade. I then asked for orders in writing. Manekshaw replied that there could be nothing in writing; no publicity and no records were to be kept. Govind Narayan concurred.

By the end of 1969, 4 and 9 Infantry Divisions and 50 Para Brigade were moved into West Bengal.

We were fortunate that the Naxalite movement was in its nascent stages and that their cadres were not well equipped. Our major concern then was the attempts by the movement to infiltrate the left wing trade unions. We took preventive action and deployed troops in sensitive factory areas and also deployed them in the mofussil areas

Unfortunately, one of the founders of the movement, Charu Mazumdar, who was coming around to negotiating table, died in police custody in July 1972.

Intensive military operations were conducted, and by mid-1971 the Naxals were driven out of West Bengal. During this period two elections were held and the army was deployed right down to the polling booths to ensure free and fair voting.

Today, the Naxal insurgency has spread to cover a large swathe of the country, from the Tarai right down to the south. The state governments with their police and paramilitary forces have not been able to deal with it. There is not enough coordination between the various states. The insurgency is gaining momentum, and the situation is one of increasing concern.

The insurgency is spreading from the forests and mofussil and tribal areas to small urban pockets and soon likely to spread to towns and cities. In certain areas, the Naxals have infiltrated government institutions. The modernization of their weaponry, their intensive training, and their intelligence gathering capability is developing rapidly. They have links with other organizations, like the Maoists in Nepal and Bhutan and other insurgents in the north east. Pakistan's ISI is also likely, in case they have not done so already, to seize the opportunity to collaborate with them.

The Naxal pattern of operations is also likely to change from the rural areas to industries to urban complexes. They are already infiltrating trade unions and government institutions. They are likely in future to increasingly target infrastructure. Possible targets are the electricity distribution system (pylons, capacitors) road and rail communications, telephone radio relay, mobile phone towers and government institutions. They are already targeting prominent politicians and officials.

The army and air force had earlier been used in the 1920s to deal with the Moplah uprising. The air force was used by the British against the Faqir of Ipi in Sind in 1940 and also to bomb Mizo rebel camps, while the army was used in West Bengal against the Naxals.

The army is currently involved in counter-insurgency operations in Jammu & Kashmir as also in the north-east. These are precedents to employ the army and air force to conduct anti-Naxal operations.

Two factors are required to keep an insurgency going strong: bases and lines of supply for money, arms and ammunition. The strong bases are in the forests, the mofussil areas, and are now spreading to the towns. In some areas, the Naxals are running a parallel government and are collecting 'taxes'. They are obtaining weapons by seizing them from the police and paramilitary, and explosives and detonators from the mines. With such access to sources of finance, weapons, and explosives, the insurgency will continue to escalate.

This notwithstanding, the government (both at the central and state levels) as well as the armed forces, are not in favour of using the military to counter the Naxals, but are we prepared to let the situation escalate further?

Shakespeare's *Hamlet* is the tragedy of procrastination. Hamlet knew what he had to do, but kept on postponing it. Let future generations not say that we are the hamlets of our age. [Earlier published in a slightly different form by sify.com]

Appendix 6: George Griffin Episode: The Spy Who Failed!

George B. Griffin was the political officer in the US Consulate in Calcutta in 1971. On 30 April 2002 he was interviewed by Stuart Charles Kennedy and in the course of this he recalled those difficult days when he was to act as messenger and reporter and try to resolve tensions between the US embassies in New Delhi and Islamabad. The interview has been released by the US Department of State ('Teaching of Diplomats') recently. Given below is an excerpt from that interview in which he speaks about his interaction with me, and specially regarding the evening when he came to my house for dinner.

> GRIFFIN: From our perspective, the Department, Embassy New Delhi, and Embassy Islamabad were squabbling about what our stance should be. In particular, Ambassadors Farland (in Islamabad) and ex-Senator Kenneth Keating (in New Delhi) seemed to us to be snarling at each other. We kept adding free advice to our reports that we should all cooperate, as we're on the same team ... One evening my wife and I were invited to supper a trois by the deputy commandant of Eastern Command, a fascinating gentleman named Major General J.F.R. Jacob. After the war he

was promoted, and became the highest ranking Jew ever in the Indian Army, something he is rightly proud of … Jackie and I got to be pretty thick after a couple of false starts. At supper that night he showed us some of his prized Chinese artifacts, and we talked a lot about art. Finally, he said, 'Don't you have to go to the bathroom? Go through the bedroom.' It took me a few moments to understand, but once in his bedroom I found a huge map of the region on his wall!

Q: A large map, yes.
GRIFFIN: … on which all of the Indian military formations were carefully plotted; all of them. I didn't have a camera, but I had a pretty good memory. I studied the map for as long as I dared, then raced to the Consulate and filed the news that there were troops where we didn't know there were troops, and many more than we had thought. Jacob was a disciple of the storied German General Heinz Guderian, who revolutionized armored warfare in World War II, and what the Indians did was rather remarkable. They took over East Pakistan almost without firing a shot. They did it by transporting an entire division across the Brahmaputra River by tank. Tanks that could swim. Soviet tanks. They did it covertly. Nobody tracked them. I guess we didn't have good real-time satellite imagery in those days, and didn't pick it up until I saw his map. It showed a whole division east of the Brahmaputra River that we didn't know about. They just rolled into Dacca one day, and that was it. The Pakistanis surrendered or fled in various ways. The Indians let some of them go without shooting them, but most were sent back to the West Wing, as it had been called before, by ship and plane.

Let me give my side of the incident now. Griffin was an affable and friendly person. I got close to him though I knew he would have to act on behalf of his bosses in the State Department. He knew the Calcutta police were keeping tabs on him but he remained friendly terms with many people in the Indian establishment. I wa, however aware that George Griffin would have pass on information to his bosses and they to their friends in Pakistan.

Things were moving rapidly in November 1971 and war with Pakistan seemed imminent. I invited Griffin and his wife for dinner at my residence. I wanted false information regarding our deployments to be sent to Pakistan. The dispositions on the map in my bedroom were accordingly altered. This I intended to be conveyed to Pakistan; the scenario was accordingly set up. Griffin accepted my dinner invitation. Griffin was most reluctant to go the bathroom. I encouraged him to go there through my bedroom where a suitably-marked map was placed there for him to see. The deception worked. He took it in hook, line and sinker. There was no division with tanks east of the Brahmaputra river. The other dispositions were also suitably entered. These were presumably conveyed by Griffin to his American bosses, and by them to their friends the Pakistanis. There were no tanks across the Brahmaputra to swim across the Brahmaputra nor were any of our tanks capable of doing so. I used Griffin, not he me. Intelligence as you well know is a many-faceted and not very pleasant business. I found Griffin to be a friendly, likable, and a cooperative. The Government of India later refused to accept his credentials in Delhi on the grounds that he was a CIA individual agent, which he was not; he was from state department. I tried to explain this to the MEA with no success [the CIA operative in Calcutta was a person called Turco].